6699

KEEPING MY WORDS

AN ANTHOLOGY OF QUOTATIONS

MAGNUS MAGNUSSON

Hodder & Stoughton
LONDON SYDNEY AUCKLAND

First published in Great Britain in 2004

The right of Magnus Magnusson to be identified as the Compiler
of the Work has been asserted by him in accordance
with the Copyright, Designs and Patents Act 1988.

10 9 8 7 6 5 4 3 2 1

British Library Cataloguing in Publication Data
A record for this book is available from the British Library

ISBN 0 340 86263 7

Typeset in Caslon by Avon DataSet Ltd,
Bidford-on-Avon, Warwickshire

Printed and bound in Great Britain by
Clays Ltd, St Ives plc

The paper used in this book is a natural recyclable product
made from wood grown in sustainable forests.
The hard coverboard is recycled.

Hodder & Stoughton
A Division of Hodder Headline Ltd
338 Euston Road
London NW1 3BH
www.madaboutbooks.com

This little family anthology of words to keep, from cradle to grave, is dedicated to my own fecund family, from the oldest to the youngest, and to those still to come.

Contents

Literary Credits

For permission to reprint copyright material the editor and publishers gratefully acknowledge the following:

Simon Campbell: Joseph Campbell, from *Complete Poems* (Allen Figgis & Co., 1963).

Carcanet Press: Robert Graves, from 'To Bring the Dead to Life', in *Complete Poems in One Volume* (2000).

Jonathan Clowes Ltd: Kingsley Amis, from *One Fat Englishman* (Victor Gollancz, 1963) and 'A Bookshop Idyll', in *Collected Poems 1944–1979* (Hutchinson, 1979).

Dee & Griffin (Solicitors): W. H. Davies, from 'School's Out', in *The Complete Poems of W. H. Davies* (Jonathan Cape, 1963).

Margo Ewart: Gavin Ewart, from 'The Sentimental Education', in *The Collected Ewart, 1933–1980* (Century, 1982).

Harvard University Press and the Trustees of Amherst College: Emily Dickinson, 'The bustle in a house', from *The Poems of Emily Dickinson*, edited by Thomas H. Johnson (Cambridge, Mass.: The Belknap Press of Harvard University Press, 1955), © 1951, 1955, 1979 by the President and Fellows of Harvard College.

David Higham Associates: Charles Causley, from 'Timothy Winters', in *Collected Poems, 1951-1975* (Macmillan, 1975); Stephen Fry, from *Paperweight* (Heinemann, 1992); Graham Greene, from *The Power and the Glory* (n.e. Penguin Books, 1991) and *A Sort of Life* (n. e. Penguin Books, 1993); Louis

MacNeice: from 'Prayer before birth', in *Collected Poems* (Faber & Faber, 1966); Malcolm Muggeridge: from *The Most of Malcolm Muggeridge* (1966); Dylan Thomas: from 'Poem in October', 'Do Not Go Gentle into that Good Night' and 'And Death Shall Have No Dominion', from *Collected Poems 1934–1952* (J. M. Dent, 1952), and *Under Milk Wood* (1954).

Jean Justice: Donald Justice, from 'Men at Forty', in *New and Selected Poems* (Alfred A. Knopf, 1995), © 1995 by Donald Justice.

Hodder Murray Publishers: John Betjeman, from *Summoned by Bells* (1960) and 'A Subaltern's Love-song', in *Collected Poems*. Enlarged Edition (1972).

Oxford University Press: Henry Reed, from 'Chard Whitlow', in *Collected Poems*, edited by Jon Stallworthy (Oxford University Press, 1991).

The Random House Group UK: Robert Frost, 'Precaution', from *Robert Frost: Selected Poems* (The Penguin Poets, 1955); Norman MacCaig, from 'Memorial', in *Collected Poems* (Chatto & Windus, 1990); W. Somerset Maugham: from *A Writer's Notebook* (Heinemann, 1949), *The Circle* (Heinemann, 1921), *Of Human Bondage* (Heinemann, 1915), *Cakes and Ale* (Heinemann, 1930), *The Summing Up* (Heinemann, 1938), an interview given on his 90th birthday, and *Conversations with Willie* (Heinemann, 1978).

The Sayle Literary Agency and the author: Ronald Searle, from *The Female Approach* (1949), © 1949 by Ronald Searle.

The Society of Authors: Laurence Binyon, from 'For the Fallen (September, 1914), published in *The Times* (1914); Walter de la Mare, 'A Child Asleep', from *Selected Poems* (Faber & Faber, 1954); A. E. Housman, from 'Poem XXXIX' in *Last Poems*, and 'Poem XXXVI', from *More Poems*, in *Collected Poems and Selected Prose* (Penguin Twentieth-Century Classics, 1991); John Masefield, from 'The Everlasting Mercy' and 'C.L.M.', in *Collected Poems* (William Heinemann, 1924); George Bernard Shaw, from *Man and Superman* (1903), *John Bull's Other Island* (1907) and other published works.

Introduction

An Introduction makes no sense until you have read the book – and then it will be irrelevant. (Anon)

For years and years I have been scribbling on scraps of paper and in dog-eared notebooks various adages, aphorisms and axioms as I came across them: wee poems, stray thoughts on life and living, *obiter dicta* and, in particular, comments and quips which caught my fancy. I have dipped with pleasure into innumerable books of quotations compiled by others. Recently I have systematised this mass of citations, under a series of some 450 headings, into an informal Commonplace Book.

❝❞

What though his head be empty, provided his commonplace book be full?

Anglo-Irish writer and clergyman **Jonathan Swift**
[1667–1745], A Tale of a Tub, Section VII

For this book I have culled a bouquet of thoughts on the
major stages of a person's life from cradle to coffin – from
embryo to eternity: in effect: conception (and preconception!),
birth, infancy, childhood, school, teachers, teenage, youth,
college, men, women, sex, love and courtship, marriage,
divorce, parents and grandparents, family and friends, middle
age, old age and death – and the whole gamut of joys and
sorrows in between.

I have tried to authenticate as many of the quotations as
possible because, regrettably, I had all too often failed to
note the source at the time. But was all the labour involved
necessary?

When a thing has been said, and well said, have no
scruple: take it and copy it. Give references? Why should
you? Either your readers know from where you have
taken the passage and the precaution is needless, or they
do not and you only humiliate them.

French novelist **Anatole France** *[1844–1924]*

Nonetheless, I have frequently had recourse to the manifold
works of Nigel Rees, the urbane host of that delightful radio
programme *Quote . . . Unquote* (and its eponymous newsletter),
and editor of the invaluable *Cassell Companion to Quotations*.
His advice is terse and to the point:

When in doubt, ascribe all quotations to George Bernard Shaw.

> *Author and broadcaster* **Nigel Rees** *[b. 1944],*
> *'Rees's First Law of Quotations' in Quote . . . Unquote 3,*
> *1983*

Dorothy Parker had another, but equally likely, catch-all candidate:

> If, with the literate, I am
> Impelled to try an epigram,
> I never seek to take the credit;
> We all assume that Oscar said it.
>
> *American writer and wit* **Dorothy Parker**
> *[1893–1967], 'Oscar Wilde'*

Everything I've ever said will be credited to Dorothy Parker.

> *Attributed to American humorist* **George S Kaufman**
> *[1889–1961]*

When all else fails, however, one can always ascribe an elusive quotation to that most prolific of all authors, 'Anon':

> I cite,
> You incorporate,
> He plagiarises.
>
> **Anon**

Some people are more honest about their use of quotations:

The difference between my quotations and those of the next man is that I leave out the inverted commas.

Attributed to Irish novelist **George Moore**
[1852–1933]

I have always been fascinated by words – all words: glutton words and starveling words, bluff words and brazen words, velvet words and gruff words, whispering words and sonorous words, soft words and cynical words, calm words and skittish words, harsh words and tender words. I love all the different ways in which people have used words down the centuries, from all kinds of backgrounds and beliefs, from so many different experiences and outlooks. That's why, for me, collecting quotations is such a rewarding pastime.

Words are wonderful. They are the symbols which reflect our understanding of the world. They tell so much. In just a few words someone can say something which is precisely what you have felt yourself but never been able to put so succinctly, so poignantly, so amusingly or so sharply. The French novelist Gustave Flaubert [1821–80] put it superbly in his *Carnets*:

Human language is like a cracked kettle on which we beat out tunes for bears to dance to, when all the time we are longing to move the stars with pity.

Quoted by novelist Graham Greene [1904–91]
in A Sort of Life, 1971

So why do people like using quotations?

Do you know, I pick up favourite quotations, and store

them in my mind as ready armour, offensive or defensive, amid the struggle of this turbulent existence.

Scottish poet **Robert Burns** *[1759–96], in a letter to Mrs Dunlop, 6 December 1792*

He wrapped himself in quotations – as a beggar would enfold himself in the purple of emperors.

Poet and novelist **Rudyard Kipling** *[1865–1936], 'The Finest Story in the World', in Many Inventions, 1893*

I quote others only the better to express myself.

French essayist **Michel de Montaigne** *[1533–92], Essays, Book 1, Chapter 26, 1580*

He rang'd his tropes, and preach'd up patience;
Back'd his opinion with quotations.

Poet and diplomat **Matthew Prior** *[1664–1721], 'Paulo Purganti and His Wife', 1708*

George Bernard Shaw was typically more brazen:

I often quote myself – it adds spice to my conversation.

Irish playwright and critic **George Bernard Shaw** *[1856–1950]*

Are you someone who likes to spice your conversation (or your writing) with quotations? You can find bouquets, brickbats and good advice in equal measure:

One must be a wise reader to quote wisely and well.

American transcendentalist **Amos Bronson Alcott**
[1799–1888] and father of Louisa May Alcott,
'Quotation', in Table Talk, 1877

Hanging is too good for a man who makes puns. He should be drawn and quoted.

American comedian **Fred Allen** *[1894–1956]*

Sometimes it seems the only accomplishment my education ever bestowed on me – the ability to think in quotations.

Novelist **Margaret Drabble** *[b. 1939], in A Summer*
Bird-Cage, 1963

By necessity, by proclivity and by delight, we all quote.

American poet and essayist **Ralph Waldo Emerson**
[1803–82], 'Quotation and Originality', in Letters
and Social Aims, 1876

The nicest thing about quotes is that they give us a nodding acquaintance with the originator which is often socially impressive.

Actor **Kenneth Williams** *[1926–88], in the preface to*
Acid Drops, 1980

Quotations can be extremely useful as off-the-peg thoughts, ready-made for instant use, and sometimes even sounding tailor-made:

I like to have quotations ready for every occasion. They give one ideas so pat, and save one the trouble of finding expressions adequate to one's feelings.

Scottish poet **Robert Burns** *[1759–96], in a letter to Mrs Agnes McLehose, 14 January 1788*

It is a good thing for an uneducated man to read books of quotations. Bartlett's *Familiar Quotations* is an admirable work, and I studied it intently. The quotations when engraved upon the memory give you good thoughts. They also make you anxious to read the authors and look for more.

Conservative Prime Minister **Winston Churchill** *[1874–1965], Roving Commission: My Early Life, 1930*

The wisdom of the wise and the experience of the ages are perpetuated by quotations.

Tory Prime Minister and novelist **Benjamin Disraeli** *[1804–81]*

Quotations are, in effect, thoughts embedded in memorable phraseology and polished by use. They are largely preformed elements and necessarily combine deep structure (the ideas) with surface structure (the actual words in which the ideas are caught). It is easy to incorporate them, like plug-in circuit boards, into one's own thinking machine.

Crystallography expert **Alan L Mackay** *[b. 1926], preface to The Harvest of a Quiet Eye: A Selection of Scientific Quotations, 1977*

I always have a quotation for everything – it saves original thinking.

> *Detective fiction writer* **Dorothy L Sayers**
> *[1893–1957], in Have His Carcase, 1932,*
> *Chapter 41, Lord Peter Wimsey to Harriet Vane*

The misuse of quotations can be a hazard for the unwary.

A fine quotation is a diamond on the finger of a man of wit, but a pebble in the hand of a fool.

> *French writer* **Joseph Roux** *[1725–93],*
> *Meditations of a Parish Priest, published in 1886*

Moth (*aside*): They have been at a great feast of languages and stol'n the scraps.
Costard: O, they have lived long on the alms-basket of words.

> *Playwright* **William Shakespeare** *[1564–1616],*
> *Love's Labour's Lost, Act 5, Scene 1, Moth and Costard*
> *talking about Holofernes, Sir Nathaniel and Dull*

> Some for renown, on scraps of learning dote,
> And think they grow immortal as they quote.
> *Poet and clergyman* **Edward Young** *[1683–1765], Love*
> *of Fame: The Universal Passion, 1725–28, Satire I*

And if you get a quotation wrong? Is that you branded for all time as a pretentious phoney? Worry not – there is a good excuse to hand:

Misquotation is, in fact, the pride and privilege of the learned. A widely-read man never quotes accurately for the rather obvious reason that he has read too widely.

Biographer **Hesketh Pearson** *[1887–1964], in the introduction to Common Misquotations, 1937*

In England only uneducated people show off their knowledge; nobody quotes Latin or Greek authors in the course of conversation, unless he has never read them.

Hungarian-born writer **George Mikes** *[1923–87], How to be an Alien, 1946*

The trouble is that quotations can all too easily become clichés through over-use – indeed, the more striking they are the more vulnerable they become.

A writer expresses himself in words that have been used before because they give his meaning better than he can give it himself, or because they are beautiful or witty, or because he expects them to touch a chord of association in his reader, or because he wishes to show that he is learned and well read. Quotations due to the last motive are invariably ill-advised; the discerning reader detects it and is contemptuous; the undiscerning is perhaps impressed, but even then is at the same time repelled, pretentious quotation being the surest way to tedium . . . To each reader those quotations are agreeable that neither strike him as hackneyed nor rebuke his ignorance.

Lexicographer **H W Fowler** *[1858–1933], A Dictionary of Modern English Usage, 1926*

An apt quotation can serve as shorthand for communicating a wealth of meaning for people with a shared culture:

> (Quotation) is a good thing; there is a community of mind in it. Classical quotation is the *parole* of literary men all over the world.
>
> *Writer and lexicographer* **Samuel Johnson** *[1709–84], quoted in Boswell's Life of Johnson, 8 May 1781*

> Quotation is a high pleasure and a password among reading people. But, as with material food, one's taste becomes more discriminating as one grows older.
>
> *Literary journalist* **Philip Howard** *[b. 1955], The State of the Language: English Observed, 1984*

For a writer, it seems that quotability can be all:

> My quarrel with him (Sir Walter Scott) is, that his works contain nothing worth quoting; and a book that furnishes no quotations is, *me judice*, no book – it is a plaything.
>
> *Novelist* **Thomas Love Peacock** *[1785–1866], Crotchet Castle, 1831, chapter 9, spoken by the Rev. Dr Folliott, conversing about the merits of 'the northern enchanter', Sir Walter Scott, compared to those of the 'southern enchanter', Charles Farley, producer of the Covent Garden pantomimes 1806–34*

It seems pointless to be quoted if one isn't going to be
quotable . . . It's better to be quotable than honest.
Playwright **Tom Stoppard** *[b. 1937], in the Guardian,*
21 March 1973

There is also a serious warning for people like me who have the
temerity to cobble together a Commonplace Book:

The majority of those who put together collections of
verses or epigrams resemble those who eat cherries or
oysters: they begin by choosing the best and end up by
eating everything.
French writer and revolutionary **Nicolas-Sébastien**
Chamfort *[1741–94], Maximes et Pensées, 1796*

Every anthologist has a favourite quote. Here's mine:

If I had a good quote, I'd be wearing it.
American singer and song-writer **Bob Dylan** *[b. 1941],*
in reply to a French journalist who asked for 'a good quote',
quoted in The Times, July 1981

This little book is a modest collection of many of the favourite
quotes which I have been wearing, on and off, for a long time.
I do not necessarily subscribe to all, or even many, of them –
but I certainly relish them. I relish the thoughts of yesteryear
which have stood the test of time, just as much as today's often
smart and iconoclastic *aperçus*. I am not a churchgoer, but I
cherish biblical quotations for their beauty, their knowledge of
life, the sonority of their certainty and their poetry. I am

delighted by quotations from children ('out of the mouths of babes and sucklings' and all that) – even the most obviously fabricated classroom howlers. And I love the hand-me-down lore from grandparents and great-grandparents, which distil the very wisdom of the ages:

> To be amused at what you read – that is the great spring of happy quotation.
> *Editor and writer* **C E Montague** *[1867–1928],*
> *A Writer's Notes on his Trade*

> You can get a happy quotation anywhere if you have the eye.
> *American jurist* **Oliver Wendell Holmes Jr**
> *[1841–1935], in a letter to Harold Laski, 31 May 1923*

The last word must go to Montaigne, in one of his *Essays*:

> It could be said of me that in this book I have only made up a bunch of other men's flowers, and provided nothing of my own but the string to bind them.
> *French essayist* **Michel de Montaigne** *[1533–92],*
> *Essays, 1580, Book 3, Chapter 12*

I make no greater claim for this little anthology, which simply means (from its Greek derivation) 'a collection of flowers'.

1

Conception – or contra

The best contraceptive is 'No'. (Anon)

In the past, most married couples assumed that having a family was the central purpose of marriage: the urge to reproduce, out of love or dynastic ambition or social imperatives, was paramount. For other, more casual couplings it was just as important *not* to conceive children. From the days of Ancient Egypt and Greece, women used primitive methods of birth control, which ranged from the application of crocodile dung and vinegar-soaked sponges to a paste containing lactic acid (a main ingredient in modern contraceptive jellies); for men, sheaths made from animal membrane and linen served as condoms from the seventeenth century onwards.

Comments about conception and birth control range from the cynical to the sentimental, from the witty to the worldly wise;

but the most strident voices are those of the post-war feminist writers, as women strove to redefine their identity. One crucial factor was the development of the oral contraceptive, the Pill, which led to what has been called 'the copulation explosion' of the 1960s and 1970s – a remarkable sexual revolution which began in San Francisco and spread like wildfire.

For every couple, starting a family is a profoundly moving experience, but most serious events can have their lighter moments, too. In this section I have included a couple of delightful classroom howlers, although I suspect that most 'classroom howlers' are composed by schoolteachers having an imaginative doodle – some of them are simply too good or too clever to ring true.

❝❞

A vasectomy means not ever having to say you're sorry.
Attributed to virtuoso harmonica player **Larry Adler**
[1914–2001]

Buy me and stop one.
Advertisement *for condoms*

I want to tell you a terrific story about oral contraception. I asked this girl to sleep with me and she said 'No'.
American film director and actor **Woody Allen** *[b. 1935],*
Woody Allen Volume Two, Colpix CP 488

The freedom women were supposed to have found in the sixties largely boiled down to easy contraception and

abortion: things to make life easier for men, in fact.
Journalist and writer **Julie Burchill** *[b. 1960],*
'Born Again Cows', in Damaged Goods, 1986

The Virgin Mary had an immaculate contraption.
Classroom howler

If you don't want babies you have to practise contra-diction.
Classroom howler

If your parents didn't have any children, there's a good chance that you won't have any.
American humorist **Clarence Day** *[1885–1933]*

By far the most common craving of pregnant women is not to be pregnant.
American comedienne **Phyllis Diller** *[1917–74]*

If men were equally at risk from this condition – if they knew that their bellies might swell as if they were suffering from end-stage cirrhosis, that they would have to go nearly a year without a stiff drink, a cigarette or even an aspirin, that they would be subject to fainting spells and unable to fight their way on to commuter trains – then I am sure that pregnancy would be classified as a sexually transmitted disease and abortions would be no more controversial than emergency appendectomies.
American feminist writer and political essayist
Barbara Ehrenreich *[b. 1941]*

If pregnancy were a book, they would cut the last two chapters.

American writer **Nora Ephron** *[b. 1941]*

Every year, in the fullness o' summer, when the sukebind hangs heavy from the wains . . . 'tes the same. And when the spring comes her hour is upon her again. 'Tes the hand of Nature and we women cannot escape it.

Novelist **Stella Gibbons** *[1902–89],*
Cold Comfort Farm, 1932, Chapter 5

The blind conviction that we have to do something about other people's reproductive behaviour, and that we may have to do it whether they like it or not, derives from the assumption that the world belongs to us who have so expertly depleted its resources, rather than to those who have not.

Australian feminist writer and academic
Germaine Greer *[b. 1939]*

Oh, what a tangled web we weave when first we practise to conceive.

American humorist **Don Herold** *[1889–1966]*

Who to the North, or South, doth set
His bed, male children shall beget.
Poet and clergyman **Robert Herrick** *[1591–1674]*

I like trying (to get pregnant). I'm not so sure about childbirth.

American film actress **Lauren Holly** *[b. 1963]*

A million million spermatozoa,
All of them alive:
Out of their cataclysm but one poor Noah
Dare hope to survive.

Poet and novelist **Aldous Huxley** *[1894–1963],*
'Fifth Philosopher's Song', 1918

If men could get pregnant, abortion would be a sacrament.

American lawyer, feminist and civil rights activist
Florynce R Kennedy *[b. 1916], 'The Verbal Karate of*
Florynce R Kennedy', in Ms, 1973

If we can get that realistic feminine morality working for us, if we can trust ourselves and so let women think and feel that an unwanted child or an oversized family is wrong – not ethically wrong, not against the rules, but morally wrong, all wrong, wrong like a thalidomide birth, wrong like taking a wrong step that will break your neck – if we can get feminine and human morality out from under the yoke of a dead ethic, then maybe we'll begin to get somewhere on the road that leads to survival.

American feminist writer **Ursula Le Guin**
[b. 1929]

It is now quite lawful for a Catholic woman to avoid pregnancy by a resort to mathematics, though she is still forbidden to resort to physics and chemistry.

American journalist and literary critic **H L Mencken**
[1880–1956], 'Minority Report', in Notebooks, 1956

Contraceptives should be used on all conceivable occasions.
Attributed to comedian **Spike Milligan** *[1918–2002],*
The Last Goon Show of All

The turtle lives 'twixt plated decks
Which practically conceal its sex.
I think it clever of the turtle
In such a fix to be so fertile.
American poet **Ogden Nash** *[1902–71], 'The Turtle',*
Many Long Years Ago, 1945

Do your kids a favour – don't have any.
American humorist **P J O'Rourke** *[b. 1947]*

Men have children to prove they aren't impotent, or at
least that some of their friends aren't.
American humorist **P J O'Rourke** *[b. 1947]*

Men are generally more careful of the breed of their
horses and dogs than of their children.
Quaker and founder of Pennsylvania **William Penn**
[1644–1718]

My best birth control now is to leave the lights on.
American comedienne **Joan Rivers** *[b. 1933]*

We want far better reasons for having children than not
knowing how to prevent them.
Feminist **Dora Russell** *[Countess Russell, 1894–1986],*
Hypatia, Chapter 4, 1925

CONCEPTION - OR CONTRA

No woman can call herself free who does not own and control her body. No woman can call herself free until she can choose consciously whether she will or will not be a mother.

American social reformer and founder of the Birth Control Movement **Margaret Sanger** *[1883–1966], Parade, 1 December 1963*

Skullion had little use for contraceptives at the best of times. Unnatural, he called them, and placed them in the lower social category of things along with elastic-sided boots and made-up bow ties. Not the sort of attire for a gentleman.

Satirical novelist **Tom Sharpe** *[b. 1928], Porterhouse Blue, 1973*

Protestant women may take the Pill. Roman Catholic women must keep taking *The Tablet*.

Writer and commentator **Irene Thomas** *[b. 1920], Guardian, 1990*

Familiarity breeds contempt – and children.

American writer **Mark Twain** *[Samuel Langhorne Clemens, 1835–1910], in Notebooks, published in 1935*

2

Birth

Man that is born of a woman is of few days, and full of trouble. (Bible, Job 14:1)

Birth must be the ultimate miracle – the miracle of nativity, of delivery, of the emergence of life, of source and origin. I cannot claim to know much about it, despite having fathered a family of five children. In the days when I got married, back in 1954, it was not customary for the father to be present at the birth of his baby. Fathers were in the way of the serious work of parturition; it was an arcane mystery, a profound temple ritual from which mere fathers were rigorously excluded. Not that I wanted to be present: I was racked with guilt over the pain which my wife must be suffering, deeply worried about what might go wrong. Although I had worked on farms since boyhood and had assisted at the births of lambs and calves and even foals, I could not relate the agricultural business of looking after livestock in labour to the birth of my own offspring.

My late brother knew all about it, however. Dr Sigurður S Magnusson (1927–85) was an obstetrician, Professor of Medicine and Head of Midwifery at the University Hospital in Iceland. He loved his work, and never lost the sense of awe which each birth he attended gave him. He often said that being a midwife was the most profoundly responsible and satisfying position which medicine had to offer.

66 99

When I was born I was so surprised I didn't talk for a year and a half.
American comedy actress **Gracie Allen** *[1895–1964]*

(Pregnancy) is a very boring time. I am not particularly maternal – it is an occupational hazard of being a wife.
HRH Anne, The Princess Royal *[b. 1950],*
in a TV interview quoted in the Daily Express, 1981

A woman when she is in travail hath sorrow, because her hour is come: but as soon as she is delivered of the child, she remembereth no more the anguish, for joy that a man is born into the world.
Bible, *John 16:21*

There are two things in this life for which we are never fully prepared, and that is twins.
American humorist **Josh Billings** *[1818–85]*

My mother groaned, my father wept,
Into the dangerous world I leapt;
Helpless, naked, piping loud,
Like a fiend hid in a cloud.

Poet and artist **William Blake** *[1757–1827],*
'Infant Sorrow', in Songs of Experience, 1794

We are not born alone. For each man, to be born is a getting to know. Every birth is getting to know.

French poet, playwright and diplomat **Paul Claudel** *[1868–1955], Traité de la Connaissance du Monde et de Soi-Même*

As soon as I stepped out of my mother's womb on to dry land, I realised that I had made a mistake – that I shouldn't have come; but the trouble with children is that they are not returnable.

Writer **Quentin Crisp** *[1908–99], The Naked Civil Servant, Chapter 2, 1968*

If men had to have babies, they would only ever have one each.

Diana, Princess of Wales *[1961–97], quoted in the Observer, 29 July 1984*

Child-bearing is glorified in part because women die from it.

American radical feminist **Andrea Dworkin** *[b. 1946]*

22

Every child is born a genius.

American architect **Buckminster Fuller**
[1895–1983]

If nature had arranged that husbands and wives should have children alternatively, there would never be more than three in a family.

American writer **Lawrence Housman**
[1865–1959]

Somewhere on this globe, every ten seconds, there is a woman giving birth to a child. She must be found and stopped.

American humorist **Sam Levenson** *[1911–80]*

Having a baby is like trying to push a grand piano through a transom.

American writer **Alice Roosevelt Longworth**
[1884–1980], quoted in Michael Teague, Mrs L, 1981

I was a test-tube baby – my star sign is Pyrex.
Scottish prison governor **Rod McCowan** *[b. 1951], at the*
Wags' Dinner in Glasgow, March 1998

Where did you come from, baby dear?
Out of the everywhere into the here.
Scottish writer and poet **George MacDonald**
[1824–1905], 'Song', in At the Back of the North Wind,
Chapter 33, 1871

I am not yet born; O fill me
with strength against those who would freeze my
humanity, would dragoon me into a lethal automaton,
would make me a cog in a machine, a thing
with one face, a thing, and against all those
who would dissipate my entirety, would
blow me like thistledown hither and
thither or hither and thither
like water held in the
hands would spill me.
Let them not make me a stone and let them not
    spill me.
Otherwise kill me.
  Poet **Louis MacNeice** *[1907–63], 'Prayer before Birth',*
                                                        1944

It is only in our advanced and synthetic civilisation that
mothers no longer sing to the babies they are carrying.
        American violinist **Yehudi Menuhin** *[1916–99],*
                quoted in the Observer, 4 January 1987

The first thing which I can record concerning myself is,
that I was born. These are wonderful words. This life, to
which neither time nor eternity can bring diminution –
this everlasting living soul, began. My mind loses itself
in these depths.
            Scottish novelist **Margaret Oliphant** *[1828–97]*

Kath: Can he be present at the birth of his child?

Ed: It's all any reasonable child can expect if the dad is present at the conception.

> *Playwright* **Joe Orton** *[1933–67], Entertaining*
> *Mr Sloane, Act 3, 1964*

Dear Mary, we all knew you had it in you.

> *American writer and wit* **Dorothy Parker** *[1893–1967],*
> *in a telegram to actress Mary Sherwood after a much-*
> *publicised pregnancy: quoted in J Keats, You Might as Well*
> *Live, 1970*

You must consider this too, that we are born, each of us, not for ourselves alone but partly for our country, partly for our parents and partly for our friends.

> *Greek philosopher* **Plato** *[c. 429–347 BC], Epistles, IX*

My obstetrician was so dumb that when I gave birth he forgot to cut the cord. For a year that kid followed me everywhere. It was like having a dog on a leash.

> *American comedienne* **Joan Rivers** *[b. 1939]*

> When we are born, we cry that we are come
> To this great stage of fools.
>
> *Playwright* **William Shakespeare** *[1564–1616],*
> *King Lear, Act 4, Scene 6, King Lear to the*
> *Earl of Gloster*

No, sure, my lord, my mother cried; but then there was a star danced, and under that was I born.

Playwright **William Shakespeare** *[1564–1616], Much Ado About Nothing, Act 2, Scene 1, Beatrice to Don Pedro*

All other occupations seem flibbertigibbety by comparison with the act of birth. Love and all its flimsy fancies are rolled under this mighty event, rolling all before it: crushed like straw conceits. Even the love of God is steam-rollered aside, as the job that must be done is done.

Canadian-born writer **Elizabeth Smart** *[1913–86], The Assumption of Rogues and Rascals, Part Four, 'Bearing', 1977*

Nothing begins, and nothing ends,
That is not paid with moan;
For we are born in other's pain,
And perish in our own.
Poet **Francis Thompson** *[1859–1907], 'Daisy', published in 1913*

I was born in very sorry circumstances. My mother was sorry and my father was sorry as well.

Comedian **Norman Wisdom** *[b. 1918], quoted in the Observer, 1998*

Our birth is but a sleep and a forgetting;
The Soul that rises with us, our life's Star,
Hath had elsewhere its setting,
And cometh from afar;
Not in entire forgetfulness,
And not in utter nakedness,
But trailing clouds of glory do we come
From God, who is our home:
Heaven lies about us in our infancy!
Poet **William Wordsworth** *[1770–1850],*
'Ode. Intimations of Immortality', 1807

Our birth is nothing but our death begun.
Poet and clergyman **Edward Young** *[1683–1765],*
Night Thoughts, 1742–46

I was so ugly when I was born, the doctor slapped my
mother.
American comedian **Henny Youngman** *[1906–97]*

3

Infancy

Prams – last year's fun on wheels. (Anon)

Baby talk – talk about babies – is the perennial topic of mothers and families the world over. Whenever mothers or grand-mothers meet, in no time at all the photographs are being brandished, the latest fond tales related, the newest infant feats relished. And little wonder. Babies are the most dramatic and demanding occurrences in a household, the objects of adoration mixed with irritation, the catalysts of domestic change and upheaval. Babies keep you awake at night, and keep you on your toes by day. Babies bring out the most tender, protective love – and the most exasperated mockery.

Motherhood – maternity – is the crucial factor in most women's natural lives. And the death of a baby, or a baby born dead, stops the heart like a blow from a sledgehammer.

""

There's only one pretty child in the world, and every mother has it.

Anon

Who breathes must suffer,
Who thinks must mourn,
And he alone is blest
Who ne'er was born.
Anon; *a note left with Child No. 734 by its mother at Coram's Foundling Hospital in the eighteenth century, quoted in John G Murray, A Gentleman Publisher's Commonplace Book, 1996*

Breast
Is best.

Anon

You see, Wendy, when the first baby laughed for the first time, the laugh broke into a thousand pieces, and they all went skipping about, and that was the beginning of fairies.

Scottish playwright **J M Barrie** *[1860–1937], in Peter Pan, Act 1, 1904*

We are all born mad. Some remain so.
Irish playwright **Samuel Beckett** *[1906–89], Waiting for Godot, Act 2*

What the mother sings to the cradle goes all the way down to the coffin.

> *American Congregationalist clergyman and writer*
> **Henry Ward Beecher** *[1813–87], Proverbs from*
> *Plymouth Pulpit, 1887*

The Angel that presided o'er my birth
Said, 'Little creature, formed of joy and mirth,
Go love without the help of any thing on earth'.

> *Poet and artist* **William Blake** *[1757–1827], 'The Angel*
> *that Presided', in Poems [written c. 1807–1809]*
> *from Blake's Note-book*

So for the mother's sake the child was dear,
And dearer was the mother for the child.

> *Poet* **Samuel Taylor Coleridge** *[1772–1834], 'Sonnet to*
> *a Friend Who Asked How I Felt When the Nurse First*
> *Presented My Infant to Me', 1797*

Every baby born into the world is a finer one than the last.

> *Novelist* **Charles Dickens** *[1812–70], Nicholas Nickleby,*
> *Chapter 8*

We spend the first twelve months of our children's lives teaching them to walk and talk, and the next twelve telling them to sit down and shut up.

> *American comedienne* **Phyllis Diller** *[1917–74]*

Lord knows what incommunicable small terrors infants go through, unknown to all. We disregard them, we say they forget, because they have not the words to make us remember . . . By the time they learn to speak they have forgotten the details of their complaints, and so we never know. They forget so quickly we say, because we cannot contemplate the fact that they never forget.

Novelist **Margaret Drabble** *[b. 1939], The Millstone,*
1965

Infancy conforms to nobody; all conform to it.

American poet and essayist **Ralph Waldo Emerson**
[1803–82], 'Self-Reliance', in Essays: First Series,
1841

Babies are such a nice way to start people.

American humorist **Don Herold** *[1889–1966]*

A loud noise at one end and no sense of responsibility at the other.

Definition of a baby, attributed to writer and Roman
Catholic priest **Ronald Knox** *[1888–1957]*

Someone would like to have you for her child
    but you are mine.
Someone would like to rear you on a costly mat
    but you are mine.
Someone would like to place you on a camel blanket
    but you are mine.
I have you to rear on a torn old mat.

Someone would like to have you as her child
but you are mine.

> **Lullaby**, *traditional: Akan (Ghana/Côte d'Ivoire),*
> *in Talking Drums, edited by Véronique Tadjo, 2000*

Hush-a-bye, baby, on the tree top,
When the wind blows the cradle will rock,
When the bough breaks the cradle will fall,
And down will come baby, cradle, and all.

> **Nursery Rhyme**, *traditional*

There is this horrible idea, beginning with Jean-Jacques
Rousseau and still going strong in college classrooms,
that natural man is naturally good . . . Anybody who's
ever met a toddler knows this is nonsense.

> *American humorist* **P J O'Rourke** *[b. 1947],*
> *Parliament of Whores*

What did my fingers do before they held him?
What did my heart do, with its love?
I have never seen a thing so clear.
His lids are like the lilac flower
And soft as a moth, his breath.
I shall not let go.
There is no guile or warp in him.
May he keep so.

> *American poet* **Sylvia Plath** *[1932–63], 'Three Women:*
> *A Poem for Three Voices', 1962*

A baby is an angel whose wings decrease as his legs increase.

Proverb – *French*

The only thing I can say about W C Fields, whom I have admired since the day he advanced upon Baby LeRoy with an ice pick, is this: any man who hates dogs and babies can't be all bad.

American writer and social scientist **Leo Rosten**
[1908–97], at a Hollywood dinner in honour of Fields,
16 February 1939

I once knew a chap who had a system of just hanging the baby on the clothes line to dry and he was greatly admired by his fellow citizens for having discovered a wonderful innovation on changing a diaper.

American writer **Damon Runyon** *[1884–1946],*
Short Takes, 1946

A baby is God's opinion that the world should go on.
American poet **Carl Sandburg** *[1878–1967]*

And one man in his time plays many parts,
His acts being seven ages. At first the infant,
Muling and puking in the nurse's arms . . .
Playwright **William Shakespeare** *[1564–1616],*
As You Like It, Act 1, Scene 7, from Jaques' 'All the world's
a stage' speech

'Do you know who made you?' 'Nobody, as I knows on,' said the child, with a short laugh. The idea seemed to amuse her considerably; for her eyes twinkled, and she added – 'I 'spect I growed. Don't think nobody ever made me'.

American writer and reformer **Harriet Beecher Stowe** *[1811–96], Uncle Tom's Cabin, Chapter 21, 1852*

A baby is an inestimable blessing and bother.

American writer **Mark Twain** *[Samuel Langhorne Clemens, 1835–1910], in a letter, 1876*

4

Childhood

Children are certain cares, but uncertain comforts.
(Proverb – English)

Childhood is – well, childhood means everything to some, and nothing to others. For myself I remember my own childhood with unalloyed pleasure, but I am sure there were some spiky bits which memory has conveniently edited out of existence. This selection of favourite quotations covers the spiky bits as well as the sweet and sentimental bits . . .

❝❞

It was no wonder that people were so horrible when they started life as children.
Novelist **Kingsley Amis** *[1922–95], One Fat Englishman, 1963*

Children's talent to endure stems from their ignorance of alternatives.

> *American writer* **Maya Angelou** *[b. 1928], in I Know*
> *Why the Caged Bird Sings, 1969, Chapter 17*

Children are natural mimics who act like their parents despite every effort to teach them good manners.

Anon

> Monday's child is fair of face,
> Tuesday's child is full of grace,
> Wednesday's child is full of woe,
> Thursday's child has far to go,
> Friday's child is loving and giving,
> Saturday's child works hard for its living,
> But a child that's born on the Sabbath day
> Is fair and wise and good and gay.

Anon

On every formal visit a child ought to be of the party, by way of provision for discourse.

> *Novelist* **Jane Austen** *[1775–1817],*
> *Sense and Sensibility, 1811*

Children sweeten labours, but they make misfortunes more bitter.

> *Courtier and philosopher* **Francis Bacon** *[1561–1626],*
> *'Of Parents and Children', in Essays, 1625*

Children have never been very good at listening to their elders, but they have never failed to imitate them. They must, they have no other models.

American writer **James Baldwin** *[1924–87],*
'Fifth Avenue, Uptown: A Letter from Harlem', in Nobody
Knows My Name, 1961

There is no sinner like a young saint.

Writer and dramatist **Aphra Behn** *[1640–89]*

> I call you bad, my little child,
> Upon the title page,
> Because a manner rude and wild
> Is common at your age.

Poet and writer **Hilaire Belloc** *[1870–1953],*
A Bad Child's Book of Beasts, Introduction, 1896

Childhood is measured out by sounds and smells
And sights, before the dark of reason grows.

Poet **John Betjeman** *[1906–84], Summoned by Bells,*
Chapter 4, 1960

The wolf also shall dwell with the lamb, and the leopard shall lie down with the kid; and the calf and the young lion and the fatling together; and a little child shall lead them.

Bible, *Isaiah 11:6*

Suffer the little children to come unto me, and forbid them not: for of such is the kingdom of God.

Bible, *Mark 10:14*

It must have been some unmarried fool that said, 'A child can ask questions that a wise man cannot answer'; because, in any decent house, a brat that starts asking questions is promptly packed off to bed.

Journalist **Arthur Binstead** *['The Pitcher', 1861–1914],
Pitcher's Proverbs, 1909*

My mother bore me in the southern wild,
And I am black, but O! my soul is white;
White as an angel is the English child:
But I am black as if bereav'd of light.

Poet and artist **William Blake** *[1757–1827], 'The Little
Black Boy', in Songs of Innocence, 1789–90*

It goes without saying that you should never have more children than you have car windows.

American humorist **Erma Bombeck** *[1927–96]*

Loving a child doesn't mean giving in to all its whims; to love him is to bring out the best in him, to teach him to love is what is difficult.

French musician and writer **Nadia Boulanger**
[1887–1970]

There is no end to the violations committed by children on children, quietly talking alone.

> *Anglo-Irish novelist and short-story writer* **Elizabeth Bowen** *[1899–1973], The House in Paris, 1935*

I always thought that once you grew up you could do anything you wanted – stay up all night or eat ice-cream straight out of the container.

> *American travel writer* **Bill Bryson** *[b. 1951], The Lost Continent, 1989*

I don't know what Scrope Davies meant by telling you I liked children, I abominate the sight of them so much that I have always had the greatest regard for the character of Herod.

> *Poet* **George, Lord Byron** *[1788–1824], in a letter, 30 August 1811*

I am fond of children (except boys).

> *Writer* **Lewis Carroll** *[Charles Lutwidge Dodgson, 1832–98], in a letter to Kathleen Eschwege, 1879*

> Speak roughly to your little boy,
> And beat him when he sneezes;
> He only does it to annoy,
> Because he knows it teases.

> *Writer* **Lewis Carroll** *[Charles Lutwidge Dodgson, 1832–98], Alice's Adventures in Wonderland, 1865*

I wouldn't be a child again. I don't know where the image of happy, laughing childhood comes from. They are a grim lot. You walk among them at your peril.

Poet and primary schoolteacher **Charles Causley**
[1917–2003]

Timothy Winters comes to school
With eyes as wide as a football-pool,
Ears like bombs and teeth like splinters:
A blitz of a boy is Timothy Winters.

Poet and primary schoolteacher **Charles Causley**
[1917–2003], 'Timothy Winters', 1957

Children are innocent and love justice. The rest of us are wicked and prefer mercy.

Novelist and essayist **G K Chesterton** *[1874–1936]*

Dear God, I am adopted. Is that as good as being real? Paul.

*From **Children's Letters to God**, Eric Marshall and Stewart Hample, 1975*

Boys do not grow up gradually. They move forward in spurts like the hands of clocks in a railway station.

Writer and critic **Cyril Connolly** *[1903–70],*
Enemies of Promise, 1938

It takes three to make a child.

American writer **e e cummings** *[1894–1962]*

Angel of Words, in vain I have striven with thee,
Nor plead a lifetime's love and loyalty;
Only, with envy, bid thee watch this face,
That says so much, so flawlessly,
And in how small a space.

> *Poet and children's writer* **Walter de la Mare**
> *[1873–1956], 'A Child Asleep'*

In the little world in which children have their
existence . . . there is nothing so finely perceived and so
finely felt as injustice.

> *Novelist* **Charles Dickens** *[1812–70], Great*
> *Expectations, 1861*

All children are essentially criminal.

> *French philosopher* **Denis Diderot** *[1713–84]*

Love children especially . . . they live to soften and purify
our hearts and, as it were, to guide us. Woe to him who
offends a child.

> *Russian novelist* **Fyodor Dostoevsky** *[1821–81],*
> *in The Brothers Karamazov, 1879–80*

It is only rarely that one can see in a little boy the promise
of a man, but one can almost always see in a little girl
the threat of a woman.

> *Attributed to French novelist* **Alexandre Dumas** *fils*
> *[1824–95]*

We find delight in the beauty and happiness of children that makes the heart too big for the body.

>*American poet and essayist* **Ralph Waldo Emerson**
>*[1803–82], 'Illusions', in The Conduct of Life,*
>*1860*

A child is a curly, dimpled lunatic.

>*American poet and essayist* **Ralph Waldo Emerson**
>*[1803–82]*

The childless escape much misery.

>*Greek playwright* **Euripides** *[c. 485–406 BC], Medea*

When children are doing nothing, they are doing mischief.

>*Novelist and judge* **Henry Fielding** *[1701–54]*

Your children are not your children.
They are the sons and daughters of Life's longing for
    itself.
They came through you but not from you
And though they are with you yet they belong not to
    you.
You may give them your love but not your thoughts,
For they have their own thoughts.
You may house their bodies but not their souls,
For their souls dwell in the house of tomorrow, which
    you cannot visit, not even in your dreams.
You may strive to be like them, but seek not to make
    them like you,

For life goes not backward nor tarries with yesterday.
You are the bows from which your children as living
    arrows are sent forth.
Syrian writer and artist **Kahlil Gibran** *[1883–1931],*
'On Children', in The Prophet, 1923

Stephen: What have you got against having children?
Simon: Well Steve, in the first place there isn't enough
room. In the second place they seem to start by mucking
up their parents' lives, and then go on in the third place
to muck up their own. In the fourth place it doesn't seem
right to bring them into a world like this. In the fifth
place and in the sixth place I don't like them very much
in the first place. OK?
Playwright **Simon Gray** *[b. 1936], Otherwise Engaged,*
Act 2

There is always one moment in childhood when the door
opens and lets the future in.
Novelist **Graham Greene** *[1904–91], The Power*
and the Glory, 1940, Part 1, Chapter 1

Child, you are like a flower,
So sweet and pure and fair.
I look at you, and sadness
Touches me with a prayer.
German poet **Heinrich Heine** *[1797–1856],*
'Du bist wie eine Blume'

The proper time to influence the character of a child is about a hundred years before he is born.

Writer and clergyman **William Ralph Inge**
[1860–1954], quoted in the Observer, 21 July 1929

One of the most obvious facts about grown-ups, to a child, is that they have forgotten what it is like to be a child.

American poet **Randall Jarrell** *[1914–65], Introduction to*
Christina Stead, The Man Who Loves Children, 1965

Allow children to be happy in their own way, for what better way will they ever find?

Writer and lexicographer **Samuel Johnson** *[1709–84],*
in a letter, 1780

Children do not give up their innate imagination, curiosity, dreaminess easily. You have to love them to get them to do that.

Scottish psychiatrist **R D Laing** *[1927–89], The Politics*
of Experience, Chapter 3, 1967

A child's a plaything for an hour.

Mary Lamb *[1775–1834], sister of Charles Lamb, in her*
brother's 'Parental Recollections', 1809

All God's children are not beautiful. Most of God's children are, in fact, barely presentable.

American writer **Fran Lebowitz** *[b. 1946],*
Metropolitan Life, 1978

Even when freshly washed and relieved of all obvious confections, children tend to be sticky.

American writer **Fran Lebowitz** *[b. 1946]*

Children are God's apostles, day by day sent forth to preach of love and hope and peace.

American poet **James Russell Lowell** *[1819–91],*
on the death of a friend's child

> And he who gives a child a treat
> Makes joy-bells ring in Heaven's street;
> And he who gives a child a home
> Builds palaces in Kingdom come.

Poet and novelist **John Masefield** *[1878–1967],*
'The Everlasting Mercy', 1911

Childhood is not from birth to a certain age and at
a certain age
The child is grown, and puts away childish things.
Childhood is the kingdom where nobody dies.
Nobody that matters, that is.

American poet **Edna St Vincent Millay** *[1892–1950],*
'Childhood is the Kingdom where Nobody Dies', in Wine
from These Grapes, 1934

I love children – especially when they cry, for then someone takes them away.

Attributed to writer **Nancy Mitford** *[1904–73]*

It should be noted that children at play are not merely playing; their games should be seen as their most serious actions.

French essayist **Michel de Montaigne** *[1533–92],*
Essays, Book 1, Chapter 23, 1580

What are little boys made of?
What are little boys made of?
Frogs and snails
And puppy-dogs' tails,
That's what little boys are made of.

What are little girls made of?
What are little girls made of?
Sugar and spice
And all that's nice,
That's what little girls are made of.

Nursery rhyme, *traditional*

Children are living jewels dropped unsustained from heaven.

Scottish poet **Robert Pollok** *[1798–1827]*

Behold the child, by Nature's kindly law,
Pleas'd with a rattle, tickled with a straw.

Poet and essayist **Alexander Pope** *[1688–1744],*
An Essay on Man, 1733

Give me a child for the first seven years, and you may do what you like with him afterwards.

Proverb, *said to be based on a Jesuit maxim*

Beat your child once a day. If you don't know why, the child does.

Proverb – *Chinese*

Children have wide ears and long tongues.

Proverb – *English*

Children are a poor man's riches.

Proverb – *English*

When children are still they have done some ill.

Proverb – *English*

Waly, waly! Bairns are bonny;
One's enough, and twa's too mony.

Proverb – *Scottish*

A child is not a vase to be filled, but a fire to be lit.

Attributed to French writer and humanist **François Rabelais** *[c. 1494–c. 1553]*

Give a little love to a child, and you get a great deal back.

Art critic **John Ruskin** *[1819–1900], The Crown of Wild Olive, Lecture 1, 1866*

How sharper than a serpent's tooth it is
To have a thankless child!
Playwright **William Shakespeare** *[1564–1616],*
King Lear, Act 1, Scene 4, King Lear, about Cordelia

I must have been an insufferable child; all children are.
Irish playwright and critic **George Bernard Shaw**
[1856–1950]

Children don't read to find their identity. They don't read to free themselves of guilt, to quench the thirst for rebellion, or to get rid of alienation. They have no use for psychology. They detest sociology . . . They still believe in good, the family, angels, devils, witches, goblins, logic, clarity, punctuation and other such obsolete stuff.
American Yiddish writer **Isaac Bashevis Singer**
[1904–91], address on receiving the Nobel Prize for
literature, Stockholm, 10 December 1978

Children nowadays love luxury, have bad manners, contempt for authority, disrespect for elders.
Greek philosopher **Socrates** *[469–399 BC]*

There are only two things a child will share willingly – communicable diseases and his mother's age.
American paediatrician **Benjamin Spock** *[1903–98],*
Dr Spock's Baby and Child Care, 1945

A child should always say what's true,
And speak when he is spoken to,
And behave mannerly at table:
At least as far as he is able.
Scottish writer **Robert Louis Stevenson** *[1850–94],*
'Whole Duty of Children', in A Child's Garden of Verses,
1885

A child's
Forgotten mornings when he walked with his mother
Through the parables
Of sunlight
And the legend of the green chapels.
Welsh poet and writer **Dylan Thomas** *[1914–53],*
'Poem in October', 1946

Children are a torment and nothing else.
Russian novelist **Leo Tolstoy** *[1828–1910]*

Children can be awe-inspiringly horrible: manipulative,
aggressive, rude, and unfeeling to a point where I often
think that, if armed, they would make up the most
terrifying fighting force the world has ever seen.
Journalist **Jill Tweedie** *[1936–93], It's Only Me, 1980*

I am convinced that, except in a few extraordinary cases,
one form or another of an unhappy childhood is essential
to the formation of exceptional gifts.
American novelist and playwright **Thornton Wilder**
[1897–1975]

The Child is Father of the Man;
And I could wish my days to be
Bound each to each by natural piety.
   Poet **William Wordsworth** *[1770–1850]*,
'My heart leaps up when I behold', in Poems, 1807

5

School

If you think education is expensive, try ignorance.
(Anon)

Do you remember 'creeping like snail unwillingly to school'?
Of course you do. We probably all do. School is one of the most
significant times of our lives – indeed, more pens have been put
to paper on the theme of schooling than on most other themes.
From time immemorial, educationists have analysed it, humor-
ists have made quips about it, philosophers have racked their
brains about it, politicians have pontificated about it. We all
have our own views, too, based on our own classroom experiences or those of our parents or our children or our grandchildren. School is a permanent field day for commentators.

❝❞

Nothing in education is so astonishing as the amount of ignorance it accumulates in the form of inert facts.

American historian and man of letters **Henry Brooks Adams** *[1838–1918], The Education of Henry Adams, Chapter 22, 1907*

My problems all started with my early education. I attended a school for emotionally disturbed teachers.

American film director and actor **Woody Allen** *[b. 1937]*

The whole object of education is . . . to develop the mind. The mind should be a thing which works.

American writer **Sherwood Anderson** *[1876–1941]*

Education should include knowledge of what to do with it.

Anon

Never let your studies interfere with your education.

Anon

The roots of education are bitter, but the fruit is sweet.

Greek philosopher **Aristotle** *[384–322 BC], quoted in Diogenes Laertes, Lives and Opinions of Eminent Philosophers*

Ask me my three main priorities for Government, and I tell you: education, education and education.

Labour Prime Minister **Tony Blair** *[b. 1953], in a speech at the Labour Party Conference, 1 October 1996. (Compare: 'What is the first part of politics? Education. The second? Education. And the third? Education',* *French historian* **Jules Michelet** *[1798–1874], in Le Peuple, 1846.)*

To go to school in a summer morn,
O! it drives all joy away;
Under a cruel eye outworn,
The little ones spend the day
In sighing and dismay.
Thank God I was never sent to school,
To be flog'd into following the style of a Fool.

Scottish clergyman and poet **Robert Blair** *[1699–1746], The Grave, 1743*

I won't say ours was a tough school, but we had our own coroner. We used to write essays like: What I'm going to be if I grow up.

American satirist **Lenny Bruce** *[1923–66]*

Example is the school of mankind, and they will learn at no other.

Irish statesman and political thinker **Edmund Burke** *[1729–97], Letters on a Regicide Peace, Letter 1*

Much knowledge is a curse.
Chinese Taoist philosopher **Chuang-Tzu** *[369–286 BC]*

I am always ready to learn, although I do not always like being taught.
Attributed to Conservative Prime Minister **Winston Churchill** *[1874–1965]*

In education there should be no class distinction.
Chinese philosopher **Confucius** *[K'ung Fu-tzu, 551–479 BC], Analects, Chapter 15*

The art of getting on at school depends on a mixture of enthusiasm with moral cowardice and social sense. The enthusiasm is for personalities and gossip about them, for a schoolboy is a novelist too busy to write.
Writer and critic **Cyril Connolly** *[1903–74], Enemies of Promise, Chapter 21, 1938*

Girls scream,
Boys shout;
Dogs bark,
School's out.
Welsh poet **W H Davies** *[1871–1940]*

EDUCATION. – At Mr Wackford Squeers' Academy, Dotheboys Hall, at the delightful village of Dotheboys, near Greta Bridge in Yorkshire, Youth are boarded, clothed, booked, furnished with pocket-money, provided with all necessaries, instructed in all languages, living and dead, mathematics, orthography, geometry, astronomy, trigonometry, the use of globes, algebra, single stick (if required), writing, arithmetic, fortification, and every other branch of classical literature. Terms, twenty guineas per annum. No extras, no vacations, and diet unparalleled.

Novelist **Charles Dickens** *[1812–70],*
Nicholas Nickleby, 1839

Education is a state-controlled manufactory of echoes.

Scottish novelist and essayist **Norman Douglas**
[1868–1952], How about Europe

Knowledge has outstripped character development, and the young today are given an education rather than an upbringing.

Soviet novelist **Ilya Ehrenburg** *[1891–1967], in 'What I*
Have Learned', Saturday Review, 30 September 1967

> Before he went to school
> he could read
> the bark of trees,
> leaf veins,
> seashell-convolutions,
> footprints,
> and the touch of fingers;
> now he goes to school,
> and he can only read words.

'**Jennifer Farley**', *in an education magazine – untraced,*
alas

Public schools are the nurseries of all vice and immorality.

> *Novelist and judge* **Henry Fielding** *[1707–54],*
> *Joseph Andrews, 1742*

Education's purpose is to replace an empty mind with an open one.

> *American art collector and publisher* **Malcolm Forbes**
> *[1919–90], in Forbes Magazine*

Education is helping the child to realize his potentialities.

> *American philosopher and psychiatrist* **Erich Fromm**
> *[1900–80]*

> Alas, regardless of their doom,
> The little victims play!
> No sense have they of ills to come,
> Nor care beyond today.

> *Poet* **Thomas Gray** *[1716–71], Ode on a Distant*
> *Prospect of Eton College, 1747*

The primary purpose of a liberal education is to make one's mind a pleasant place in which to spend one's leisure.

> *American journalist* **Sydney J Harris** *[1917–86]*

A school should not be a preparation for life. A school should be life.

> *American writer and editor* **Elbert Hubbard**
> *[1856–1915]*

The aim of education is the knowledge not of facts but of values.

Writer and Dean of St Paul's **William Ralph Inge**
[1860–1954], 'The Training of the Reason', in Cambridge
Essays on Education, edited by A C Benson, 1917

At the desk where I sit, I have learned one great truth. The answer for all our national problems – the answer for all the problems of the world – comes to a single word. That word is 'education'.

US President **Lyndon B Johnson** *[1908–73]*

The supreme end of education is expert discernment in all things – the power to tell the good from the bad, the genuine from the counterfeit, and to prefer the good and the genuine to the bad and the counterfeit.

Writer and lexicographer **Samuel Johnson** *[1709–84]*

A child miseducated is a child lost.

US President **John F Kennedy** *[1917–63]*

School days, I believe, are the unhappiest in the whole span of human existence. They are full of dull, unintelligible tasks, new and unpleasant ordinances, brutal violations of common sense and common decency.

American journalist and literary critic **H L Mencken**
[1880–1956], 'Travail', in The Baltimore Evening Sun,
8 October 1928

Oh, children, growing up to be
Adventurers into sophistry,
Forbear, forbear to be of those
That read the rood to learn the rose.
American poet **Edna St Vincent Millay** *[1892–1950],*
in Mine the Harvest, 1954

And if education is always to be conceived along the same antiquated lines of a mere transmission of knowledge, there is little to be hoped from it in the bettering of man's future. For what is the use of transmitting knowledge if the individual's total development lags behind?
Italian educationist and physician **Maria Montessori**
[1870–1952], The Absorbent Mind, 1911

In the education of children there is nothing like alluring the interest and affection; otherwise you only make so many asses laden with books.
French essayist **Michel de Montaigne** *[1533–92]*

At school I never minded the lessons. I just resented having to work terribly hard at playing.
Novelist and playwright **John Mortimer** *[b. 1923],*
A Voyage Round My Father, Act 1, 1971

I hold very strongly that the first step in intellectual training is to impress upon a boy's mind the idea of science, method, order, principle and system; of rule and exception; of richness and harmony. However, it is so easy to crush a nascent sensibility or, if not to crush it, then to deform it. The poetic sensibility is especially vulnerable.

Cardinal and poet **John Henry Newman**
[1901–90], quoted by Sir Herbert Read in The Contrary
Experience

Casting Out Fear ought to be the motto over every school door.

Scottish educationist and founder of Summerhill School
A S Neill *[1883–1973], The Problem Child, 1926*

One of the things you learn from talking to today's youngsters is that schools seem to be dropping education from the curriculum.

American comedian and speech-writer **Bob Orben**
[b. 1927]

'Tis education forms the common mind,
Just as the twig is bent, the tree's inclined.

Poet and essayist **Alexander Pope** *[1688–1744],*
'To Lord Cobham', in Epistles to Several Persons,
1734

(The 11–plus) split me from a girl I carried a torch for. She passed, I failed. She went to grammar school. I sent her a love letter telling her I missed her – she sent it back with the spelling mistakes corrected.

Labour politician **John Prescott** *[b. 1938], in 1996*

I hear and I forget. I see and I remember. I do and I understand.

Proverb – *Chinese*

If you plan for a year, plant a seed. If for ten years, plant a tree. If for a hundred years, build a school.

Proverb – *Chinese*

Every school needs a debating society far more than it needs a computer. For a free society, it is essential.

Scots-born Conservative politician **Malcolm Rifkind** *[b. 1946], in A Scottish Childhood, Volume I, edited by Kamm and Lean, 1985*

Try not to have a good time . . . This is supposed to be educational.

American cartoonist **Charles M Schulz** *[1922–2000], 'Peanuts' comic strip*

Do you know the difference between education and experience? Education is when you read the fine print; experience is what you get when you don't.

American song-writer and folk-singer **Pete Seeger** *[b. 1919], quoted in Loose Talk, edited by L Botts, 1980*

And then the whining schoolboy, with his satchel,
And shining morning face, creeping like snail
Unwillingly to school.

Playwright **William Shakespeare** *[1564–1616],*
As You Like It, Act 2, Scene 7, part of Jaques' 'All the
world's a stage' speech

Me having no education, I had to use my brains.

Scottish football manager **Bill Shankly** *[1914–81],*
quoted in 'Tips from the Top', Caledonia, June 2002

What we want is to see the child in pursuit of knowledge,
and not knowledge in pursuit of the child.

Irish playwright and critic **George Bernard Shaw**
[1856–1950]

I have never let my schooling interfere with my
education.

American writer **Mark Twain** *[Samuel Langhorne*
Clemens, 1835–1910]

The Founding Fathers in their wisdom decided that
children were an unnatural strain on parents. So they
provided jails called schools, equipped with tortures
called an education. School is where you go between
when your parents can't take you and industry can't take
you.

American writer **John Updike** *[b. 1932],*
The Centaur, Chapter 4

61

If I had learned education I would not have had time to learn anything else.

American businessman **Cornelius Vanderbilt**
[1794–1877]

Education is an admirable thing, but it is well to remember from time to time that nothing that is worth knowing can be taught.

Irish playwright and wit **Oscar Wilde** *[1854–1900],*
The Critic as Artist, 1890

6
Teachers

To teach is to touch lives forever. (Anon)

Most of us, I am sure, remember at least one of our teachers – with affection, with respect or with awe: the person who had the greatest effect on us, either through inspiration or (less frequently, I hope) through fear. That teacher's influence may not have been apparent at the time, but it comes to be appreciated more and more as time goes by...

❝❞

A teacher affects eternity; he can never tell where his influence ends.

American historian and man of letters **Henry Brooks Adams** *[1838–1918], The Education of Henry Adams, Chapter 20, 1907*

The true teacher defends his pupils against his own personal influence. He inspires self-trust. He guides their eyes from himself to the spirit that quickens him. He will have no disciple.

American transcendentalist **Amos Bronson Alcott** *[1799–1888], 'The Teacher', in Orphic Sayings from the Dial, July 1840*

To know how to suggest is the great art of teaching.

Swiss philosopher and writer **Henri Frédéric Amiel** *[1821–81]*

The secret of teaching is to appear to have known all your life what you only learned this afternoon.

Anon

Those who know, do; those who understand, teach.

Greek philosopher **Aristotle** *[384–322 BC]*

For rigorous teachers seized my youth,
And purged its faith, and trimmed its fire,
Showed me the high, white star of Truth,
There bade me gaze, and there aspire.
> Poet and essayist **Matthew Arnold** [1822–88],
> 'Stanzas from the Grande Chartreuse', 1855

Teaching is not a lost art, but the regard for it is a lost tradition.
> American historian and educationist **Jacques Barzun**
> [b. 1907]

The method of teaching which approaches most nearly to the method of investigation is incomparably the best.
> Irish statesman and political thinker **Edmund Burke**
> [1729–97]

That is the difference between good teachers and great teachers: good teachers make the best of a pupil's means; great teachers foresee a pupil's ends.
> American operatic soprano **Maria Callas** [1923–77],
> quoted in Kenneth Harris Talking to: Maria Callas

It were better to perish than to continue schoolmastering.
> Scottish historian and philosopher **Thomas Carlyle**
> [1795–1881], cited in Wilson, Carlyle Till Marriage,
> 1923

'We called him Tortoise because he taught us,' said the Mock Turtle angrily. 'Really you are very dull.'

Writer **Lewis Carroll** *[Charles Lutwidge Dodgson, 1832–98], Alice's Adventures in Wonderland, 1865*

And gladly wolde he lerne and gladly teche.

Poet **Geoffrey Chaucer** *[c. 1345–1400], The Canterbury Tales, General Prologue, referring to the Clerk*

Headmasters have powers at their disposal with which Prime Ministers have never yet been invested.

Conservative Prime Minister **Winston Churchill** *[1874–1965], My Early Life, Chapter 2, 1930*

The position as master or mistress in the classroom should be recognised by society and should be given the necessary authority and suitable resources.

French Socialist politician **Jacques Delors** *[b. 1925]*

Now, what I want is, Facts. Teach these boys and girls nothing but Facts. Facts alone are wanted in life. Plant nothing else, and root out everything else. You can only form the minds of reasoning animals upon Facts: nothing else will ever be of any service to them. This is the principle on which I bring up my own children, and this is the principle on which I bring up these children. Stick to Facts, Sir!

Novelist **Charles Dickens** *[1812–70], Hard Times, spoken by the schoolmaster Thomas Gradgrind – 'A man of realities. A man of facts and calculations'*

The secret of education lies in respecting the pupil.
American poet and essayist **Ralph Waldo Emerson**
[1803–82]

Charming women can true converts make,
We love the precepts for the teacher's sake.
Irish playwright **George Farquhar** *[1678–1707],*
The Constant Couple, 1699

The whole art of teaching is only the art of awakening
the natural curiosity of young minds for the purpose of
satisfying it afterwards.
French novelist **Anatole France** *[1844–1924],*
The Crime of Sylvestre Bonnard, 1881

Let schoolmasters puzzle their brain,
With grammar, and nonsense, and earning,
Good liquor, I stoutly maintain,
Gives genius a better discerning.
Irish-born writer and playwright **Oliver Goldsmith**
[1728–74], She Stoops to Conquer, Act 1

Everyone who remembers his own educational experience remembers teachers, not methods and techniques.
American educationist and philosopher **Sidney Hook**
[1902–89]

The object of teaching a child is to enable him to get along without a teacher.

American writer and editor **Elbert Hubbard**
[1856–1915]

The child will always attend more to what a teacher does than to what the same teacher says.

American psychologist **William James** *[1842–1910],*
Talks to Teachers

One looks with appreciation to the brilliant teachers, but with gratitude to those who touched our human feelings. The curriculum is so much necessary raw material, but warmth is the vital element for the growing plant and for the soul of the child.

Swiss psychiatrist **Carl Jung** *[1875–1961]*

Nothing would more effectively further the cause of education than for all flogging pedagogues to learn to educate with the head instead of with the hand.

Swedish feminist writer **Ellen Key** *[1849–1926],*
The Century of the Child, Chapter 3

To be a teacher in the right sense is to be a learner.

Danish philosopher and theologian **Søren Kierkegaard**
[1813–55]

One learns more from a good scholar in a rage than from a score of lucid and laborious drudges.

Poet and novelist **Rudyard Kipling** *[1865–1936]*

I owe a lot to my teachers and mean to pay them back some day.

> *Canadian economist and humorist* **Stephen Leacock**
> *[1869–1944]*

Learning, I think, is the least part of education.

> *Empiricist philosopher* **John Locke** *[1632–1704]*

What I want to achieve is a position where the man in the woolly sweater and the battered sedan and the grimy house at the corner of the street is not the local teacher.

> *Conservative Prime Minister* **John Major** *[b. 1942],*
> *in 1990*

The average schoolmaster is and always must be essentially an ass, for how can one imagine an intelligent man engaging in so puerile an avocation.

> *American journalist and literary critic* **H L Mencken**
> *[1880–1956]*

We teachers can only help the work going on, as servants wait upon a master.

> *Italian educationist and physician* **Maria Montessori**
> *[1870–1952], The Absorbent Mind, Collected Lectures,*
> *1988*

Every schoolmaster after the age of 49 is inclined to flatulence, is apt to swallow frequently, and to puff.

> *Writer and diplomat* **Harold Nicolson** *[1886–1968],*
> *The Old School*

Liberals have invented whole college majors – psychology, sociology, women's studies – to prove that nothing is anybody's fault.

American humorist **P J O'Rourke** *[b. 1947],*
Give War a Chance, 1992

The schoolteacher is certainly underpaid as a childminder, but ludicrously overpaid as an educator.

Playwright **John Osborne** *[1929–94], quoted in the*
Observer, 21 July 1985

> We don't need no education.
> We don't need no thought control.
> No dark sarcasm in the classroom.
> Hey! Teacher! Leave them kids alone.

Pop group **Pink Floyd**, *'Another Brick in The Wall', 1979*
– their only No 1 UK hit song

Teachers open the door. You enter by yourself.

Proverb *– Chinese*

Experience is the best teacher.

Proverb *– English*

Better than a thousand days of diligent study is one day with a great teacher.

Proverb *– Japanese*

The test of a good teacher is not how many questions he can ask his pupils that they will answer readily, but how many questions he inspires them to ask him which he finds it hard to answer.

American novelist and critic **Alice Wellington Rollins**
[1847–97]

A teacher is like a candle which lights others in consuming itself.

Italian writer **Giovanni Ruffini** *[1807–81]*

Passive acceptance of the teacher's wisdom is easy to most boys and girls. It involves no effort of independent thought, and seems rational because the teacher knows more than his pupils; it is moreover the way to win the favour of the teacher unless he is a very exceptional man.

Philosopher and mathematician **Bertrand Russell**
[1872–1970]

Teachers open our eyes to the world. They give us curiosity and confidence. They teach us to ask questions. They connect us to our past and future. They are the guardians of our social heritage ... Life without a teacher is simply not a life.

Chief Rabbi **Jonathan Sacks** *[b. 1948]*

For every person wishing to teach there are approximately thirty who don't want to learn – much.

> *Humorous writers* **W C Sellar** and **R J Yeatman**
> *[1898–1951 and 1897–1968], And Now All This,*
> *Introduction, 1932*

It is when the gods hate a man with uncommon abhorrence that they drive him into the profession of a schoolmaster.

> *Roman philosopher and poet* **Seneca** *[c. 4 BC–AD 65],*
> *Epistolae ad Lucilium, AD 64*

He who can, does. He who cannot, teaches.

> *Irish playwright and critic* **George Bernard Shaw**
> *[1856–1950], Man and Superman, 1903; 'Maxims for*
> *Revolutionists' was included with the published text*

To me, education is a leading out of what is already there in the pupil's soul. To Miss Mackay it is a putting in of something that is not there, and that is not what I call education, I call it intrusion . . .

> *Scottish novelist* **Muriel Spark** *[b. 1918], The Prime of*
> *Miss Jean Brodie, 1961*

Give me a girl at an impressionable age, and she is mine for life.

> *Scottish novelist* **Muriel Spark** *[b. 1918], The Prime of*
> *Miss Jean Brodie, 1961*

A teacher should have maximal authority and minimal power.

Hungarian-born American psychiatrist **Thomas Szasz**
[b. 1920], 'Education', in The Second Sin, 1973

I like a teacher who gives you something to take home to think about besides homework.

American comic actress **Lily Tomlin** *('Edith Ann',*
b. 1939)

The art of teaching is the art of assisting discovery.

American poet and critic **Mark van Doren**
[1894–1972]

The mediocre teacher tells. The good teacher explains. The superior teacher demonstrates. The great teacher inspires.

American educationist and author **William Arthur Ward**
[1921–94]

I expect you'll be becoming a schoolmaster, sir. That's what most of the gentlemen does, sir, that gets sent down for indecent behaviour.

Novelist **Evelyn Waugh** *[1903–66], Decline and Fall,*
Prelude, 1928

Everyone who is incapable of learning has taken to teaching.

Irish playwright and wit **Oscar Wilde** *[1854–1900],*
'The Decay of Lying', 1889

7

Teenage

Kids used to ask where they came from; now they tell you where to go. (Anon)

Fifty years ago they did not even exist – or, at least, they were in disguise. I am talking about 'teenagers', because the word had scarcely been invented then. In those days we used to call them 'adolescents', derived from the Latin verb *adolescere*, to grow up. 'Teenager' was an inspired neologism; it was based, of course, on all the '-teens' between thirteen and nineteen; I used to call them 'tweenagers' instead, because they are between childhood and adulthood. Over the past fifty years, 'teenage' has been a useful label for the profound hormonal changes which afflict growing children as they enter puberty – and which seem to arrive earlier and earlier, compared to my days as a youngster. Teenagers quickly formed a distinct social sub-class, a separate commercial target for pop culture produce and all its relentless by-products. A recent survey revealed that 16-year-olds in the UK had an average spending power of £3,000 a year – a combined spend of £2 billion annually. Teenage is still one of the most confusing, worrying and anxiety-racked periods in a person's life. But at least they grow out of it, in time.

66 99

Adolescence: a stage between infancy and adultery.

Anon

Adolescence is a period of rapid changes. Between the ages of twelve and seventeen, for example, a parent ages as much as twenty years.

Anon

There's nothing wrong with teenagers which reasoning with them won't aggravate.

Anon

What a cunning mixture of sentiment, pity, tenderness, irony surrounds adolescence, what knowing watchfulness! Young birds on their first flight are hardly so hovered around.

French priest and writer **George Bernarnos**
[1888–1948], The Diary of a Country Priest, 1936

You don't have to suffer to be a poet. Adolescence is enough suffering for anyone.

Attributed to American poet **John Ciardi** *[1916–86]*

The young always have the same problem – how to rebel and conform at the same time. They have now solved this by defying their parents and copying one another.

English writer **Quentin Crisp** *[b. 1908], in The Naked Civil Servant, 1968*

The big mistake that men make is that when they turn thirteen or fourteen and all of a sudden they've reached puberty, they believe that they like women. Actually, you're just horny. It doesn't mean you like women any more at twenty-one than you did at ten.

American cartoonist **Jules Feiffer** *[b. 1929]*

They mustn't know my despair, I can't let them see the wounds which they have caused, I couldn't bear their sympathy and their kind-hearted jokes, it would only make me want to scream all the more. If I talk, everyone thinks I'm showing off; when I'm silent they think I'm ridiculous; rude if I answer, sly if I get a good idea, lazy if I'm tired, selfish if I eat a mouthful more than I should, stupid, cowardly, crafty, etc. etc.

German-born teenage diarist **Anne Frank** *[1929–45], Diary of a Young Girl*

Adolescents tend to be passionate people, and passion is no less real because it is directed towards a hot-rod, a commercialised popular singer, or the leader of a black-jacketed gang.

Canadian educationist and sociologist **Edgar Z Friedenberg** *[b. 1921], 'Emotional Development in Adolescence', in The Vanishing Adolescent, 1959*

Boys will be boys. And even that wouldn't matter if only we could prevent girls from being girls.

Novelist **Anthony Hope** *[1863–1933]*

The imagination of a boy is healthy, and the mature imagination of a man is healthy; but there is a space of life in between, in which the soul is in a ferment, the character undecided, the way of life uncertain, the ambition thick-sighted: thence proceeds mawkishness.

Poet **John Keats** *[1795–1821], Preface to Endymion, 1818*

Remember that as a teenager you are at the last stage in your life when you will be happy to hear that the phone is for you.

American writer **Fran Lebowitz** *[b. 1946], 'Tips for Teens', in Social Studies, 1981*

Adolescence is like cactus.

French-born American writer **Anaïs Nin** *[1903–77]*

You know your children are growing up when they stop asking you where they came from and refuse to tell you where they're going.

American humorist **P J O'Rourke** *[b. 1947]*

I keep looking back, as far as I can remember, and I can't think what it was like to feel young, really young.

Playwright **John Osborne** *[1929–94], Look Back in Anger, 1956*

The ripeness of adolescence is prodigal in pleasures, skittish, and in need of a bridle.

Greek philosopher and biographer **Plutarch** *[AD 46–c. 120], 'The Education of Children', in Moralia*

So much of adolescence is an ill-defined dying,
An intolerable waiting,
A longing for another place and time,
Another condition.

American poet **Theodore Roethke** *[1908–63], 'I'm Here', in The Collected Verse of Theodore Roethke, 1961*

I would there were no age between ten and three and twenty, or that youth would sleep out the rest; for there is nothing in the between but getting wenches with child, wronging the ancientry, stealing, fighting.

Playwright **William Shakespeare** *[1564–1616], The Winter's Tale, Act 3, Scene 3, the old shepherd speaking to Antigonus*

Don't laugh at a youth for his affectations; he is only trying on one face after another to find a face of his own.

American-born British writer **Logan Pearsall Smith**
[1865–1946], Afterthoughts, 1931

8

Youth

There is nothing wrong with the younger generation which the older generation did not outgrow. (Anon)

Ah, youth! For most people, youth represents a past often viewed through rose-tinted spectacles – nostalgia as a kind of selective amnesia. Youth is present fun and joy, a time of unlimited ambition, an infinitely promising threshold to the future. Depending on what that future brought, hindsight lends youth either a golden glow or a haze of bitter regret. Wasn't it great to be young – or else, what on earth did we do with our youth? Did we catch the bus, or miss the boat? Some remain young all their lives, others are old before their time. 'Time', as always, is the key concept as we journey from the cradle to the grave.

66 99

You are only young once, but you can stay immature indefinitely.

Anon

Youth would be an ideal state if it came a little later in life.

Liberal Prime Minister **Herbert Asquith** *[1852–1928],*
Observer, 15 April 1923

The secret of staying young is to live honestly, eat slowly and lie about your age.

American actress **Lucille Ball** *[1910–89]*

I am not young enough to know everything.

Scottish playwright **J M Barrie** *[1860–1937]*

Rejoice, O young man, in thy youth; and let thy heart cheer thee in the days of thy youth.

Bible, *Ecclesiastes 11:9*

Remember now thy Creator in the days of thy youth, while the evil days come not, nor the years draw nigh, when thou shalt say, I have no pleasure in them.

Bible, *Ecclesiastes 12:1*

Youth is the only season for enjoyment, and the first twenty-five years of one's life are worth all the rest of the longest life of man, even though those five-and-twenty be spent in penury and contempt, and the rest in the possession of wealth, honours, respectability.

Writer **George Borrow** *[1803–81], The Romany Rye,*
Chapter 30, 1857

Such, such were the joys,
When we all girls and boys,
In our youth time were seen,
On the Echoing Green.
Poet and artist **William Blake** *[1757–1827],*
'The Echoing Green', in Songs of Innocence, 1789

You haven't truly grown up until your parents have stopped embarrassing you.

Writer **Alan Brien** *[b. 1925]*

The young do not know enough to be prudent, and therefore they attempt the impossible, and achieve it, generation after generation.

American novelist **Pearl S Buck** *[1892–1973]*

Oh, talk not to me of a name great in story;
The days of our youth are the days of our glory;
And the myrtle and ivy of sweet two-and-twenty
Are worth all your laurels, though ever so plenty.
Poet **George, Lord Byron** *[1788–1824], 'Stanzas Written*
on the Road between Florence and Pisa', November 1821

Youth is something very new: twenty years ago no one mentioned it.

French couturière **Coco Chanel** *[1883–1971], in Coco Chanel, Her Life, her Secrets, by Marcel Haedrich, 1971*

To pass our youth in dull indifference, to refuse the sweets of life because they once must leave us, is as preposterous as to wish to have been born old because we one day must be old. For my part, my youth may wear and waste, but it shall never rust in my possession.

Playwright **William Congreve** *[1670–1729], The Way of the World, Act 1, Scene 1, Mrs Marwood talking to Mrs Fainall*

I remember my youth and the feeling that will never come back any more – the feeling that I could last for ever, outlast the sea, the earth, and all men; the deceitful feeling that lures us on to joys, to perils, to love, to vain effort – to death; the triumphant conviction of strength, the heat of life in the handful of dust, the glow in the heart that with every year grows dim, grows cold, grows small, and expires – and expires, too soon, too soon – before death itself.

Polish-born English novelist **Joseph Conrad** *[1857–1924], Youth, 1902*

We must prepare for the coming hour. The claims of the future are represented by suffering millions and the Youth of a Nation are the trustees of Posterity.

Tory Prime Minister and novelist **Benjamin Disraeli** *[1804–81], the closing words of Sybil, 1845*

Almost everything that is great has been done by youth.
Tory Prime Minister and novelist **Benjamin Disraeli**
[1804–81], Coningsby, 1844

A man who is not a liberal at sixteen has no heart; a man
who is not a conservative at sixty has no head.
Attributed to Tory Prime Minister and novelist **Benjamin**
Disraeli *[1804–81] but others have said something*
similar, such as French Prime Minister **Georges**
Clemenceau *[1841–1929] and clergyman and theologian*
Dean **William Inge** *[1860–1954]*

If youth but knew, if old age but could. – *Si jeunesse*
savait, si vieillesse pouvait
French printer and publisher **Henri Estienne**
[1531–98], in Les Prémices, 1594, Book 4, Epigram 4

Alas, that Spring should vanish with the Rose!
That Youth's sweet-scented Manuscript should close!
The Nightingale that in the Branches sang,
Ah, whence, and whither flown again, who knows!
Poet **Edward Fitzgerald** *[1809–93], The Rubáiyát of*
Omar Khayyám, 1879

At twenty years of age, the will reigns; at thirty, the wit;
and at forty, the judgement.
American politician and scientist **Benjamin Franklin**
[1706–90], Poor Richard's Almanack, 1736

I never dared to be radical when young
For fear it would make me conservative when old.
American poet **Robert Frost** *[1874–1963]*

This is a youth-orientated society, and the joke is on them
because youth is a disease from which we all recover.
American newscaster and writer **Dorothy Fuldheim**
[1893–1989], in A Thousand Friends, 1974

Youth's the season made for joys;
Love is then our duty.
Poet and dramatist **John Gay** *[1685–1732],*
The Beggar's Opera, 1728

Now that the April of your youth adorns
The garden of your face.
Philosopher and poet **Lord Herbert of Cherbury**
[1583–1648], 'Ditty: Now that the April',
1665

Gather ye rosebuds while ye may,
Old Time is still a-flying;
And this same flower that smiles today
Tomorrow will be dying.

The glorious lamp of heaven, the Sun,
The higher he's a-getting,
The sooner will his race be run,
And nearer he's to setting.

That age is best which is the first,
When youth and blood are warmer;
But being spent, the worse, and worst
Times, still succeed the former.

Then be not coy, but use your time,
And while ye may, go marry:
For having lost but once your prime,
You may for ever tarry.
Poet and clergyman **Robert Herrick** *[1591–1674],*
in To the Virgins, to Make Much of Time,
1648

Young men have more virtue than old men; they have
more generous sentiments in every sense.
Writer and lexicographer **Samuel Johnson** *[1709–84],*
in Boswell's The Life of Samuel Johnson,
1791

Young men make great mistakes in life; for one thing,
they idealise love too much.
Classicist and Oxford don **Benjamin Jowett** *[1817–93],*
Life and Letters of Benjamin Jowett, 1897

When all the world is young, lad,
And all the trees are green;
And every goose a swan, lad,
And every lass a queen;
Then hey for boot and horse, lad,
And round the world away:

Young blood must have its course, lad,
And every dog his day.
Novelist and poet **Charles Kingsley** *[1819–75],*
The Water Babies, 1863, song 'Young and Old'

Youth had been a habit of hers for so long that she could not part with it.
Poet and novelist **Rudyard Kipling** *[1865–1936]*

Between twenty-five and thirty-five you're too young to do anything well; after thirty-five you're too old.
American violinist **Fritz Kreisler** *[1875–1962]*

Youth is vivid rather than happy, but memory always remembers the happy things.
Astronomer **Bernard Lovell** *[b. 1913], quoted in*
The Times, 20 August 1993

There is a fountain of youth: it is your mind, your talents, the creativity you bring to your life and to the lives of the people you love. When you learn to tap this source, you will have truly defeated age.
Italian film actress **Sophia Loren** *[b. 1934]*

If youth be a defect, it is one that we outgrow only too soon.
American poet **James Russell Lowell** *[1819–91]*

In the lexicon of youth, which Fate reserves
For a bright manhood, there is no such word
As – 'fail'!
Politician and playwright **Edward Bulwer Lytton**
[1803–73], Richelieu, 1839

The atrocious crime of being a young man, which the honourable gentleman (Sir Robert Walpole) has, with such spirit and decency, charged upon me, I shall neither attempt to palliate nor deny; but I content myself with wishing that I may be one of those whose follies cease with their youth, and not of those who continue ignorant in spite of age and experience.
Whig Prime Minister **William Pitt the Elder**
[First Earl of Chatham, 1708–78], in the House of Commons, 6 March 1741

Yes, I know I am young and inexperienced but it is a fault I am remedying every day.
Whig Prime Minister **William Pitt the Younger**
[1759–1806]; he had become Prime Minister at the age of twenty-four

How ruthless and hard and vile and right the young are.
Australian playwright and poet **Hal Porter** *[1911–84], The Watcher on the Cast-iron Balcony, 1963*

Prepare in youth for your old age.
Proverb – *Yiddish*

The young have aspirations that never come to pass, the old have reminiscences of what never happened.

> *Scottish writer* **Saki** *[H H Munro, 1870–1916],*
> *'Reginald at the Carlton', 1904*

What is love? 'tis not hereafter;
Present mirth hath present laughter;
What's to come is still unsure:
In delay there lies no plenty;
Then come kiss me, sweet and twenty,
Youth's a stuff will not endure.

> *Playwright* **William Shakespeare** *[1564–1616], Twelfth*
> *Night, Act 2, Scene 3, the Clown sings for*
> *Sir Andrew Aguecheek and Sir Toby Belch*

Youth is a wonderful thing. What a crime to waste it on the young.

> *Attributed to Irish playwright and critic* **George Bernard**
> **Shaw** *[1856–1950], but possibly derived from*
> *Oscar Wilde*

What music is more enchanting than the voices of young people, when you can't hear what they say?

> *American-born British writer* **Logan Pearsall Smith**
> *[1865–1946], in Afterthoughts, 1931*

To play billiards well is the sign of a misspent youth.

> *Philosopher* **Herbert Spenser** *[1820–1903],*
> *probably quoting Robert Louis Stevenson in the Billiards*
> *Room at the Savile Club in London*

Youth is the time to go flashing from one end of the world to the other both in mind and body; to try the manners of different nations; to hear the chimes at midnight; to see sunrise in town and country; to be converted at a revival; to circumnavigate the metaphysics, write halting verses, run a mile to see a fire, and wait all day long in the theatre to applaud *Hernani*.

Scottish writer **Robert Louis Stevenson** *[1850–94]*,
Virginibus Puerisque, 1881

In youth alone, unhappy mortals live;
But oh! the mighty bliss is fugitive.
Discoloured sickness, anxious labours, come,
And age and death's inexorable doom.
Roman poet **Virgil** *[70–19 BC], The Georgics*

Youth, large, lusty, loving – youth full of grace, force, fascination,
Do you know that Old Age may come after you with equal grace, force, fascination?

American poet and writer **Walt Whitman**
[1819–1924], 'Youth, Day, Old Age and Night', 1855

The old-fashioned respect for the young is fast dying out.

Irish playwright and wit **Oscar Wilde** *[1854–1900]*,
The Importance of Being Earnest, 1895

Oh! pleasant exercise of hope and joy!
For mighty were the auxiliars which then stood
Upon our side, we who were strong in love!
Bliss was it in that dawn to be alive,
But to be young was very heaven!

Poet **William Wordsworth** *[1770–1850], the opening
lines of 'The French Revolution, as it Appeared to
Enthusiasts at its Commencement', 1809; the lines also
appear in The Prelude, Book 9, 1850*

9

College and university

A lecture is a process by which the notes of the professor become the notes of the students without passing through the minds of either. (Anon)

Colleges and universities are undergoing tremendous changes nowadays. Since the Second World War, the number of universities in Britain has soared, as polytechnics and other specialised colleges have been upgraded to university status. Britain wants to see at least 50 per cent of all school-leavers go on to higher education (Scotland has already beaten that target with 52 per cent). It has led to cheap sneers about the awarding of 'Mickey Mouse' degrees, in plumbing or embroidery, which reflect the lingering social snobbery of the old compartmentalised university system. As the Chancellor of one of Scotland's youngest universities – Glasgow Caledonian University, founded in 1993 – I have a particular interest in this huge expansion; 'Glasgow Caley' was set up with a mission to target youngsters whose families have never had any experience of university or college, and so far it has been a huge success. But the old shibboleths die hard . . .

66 99

'Whom are you?' he said, for he had attended business college.

American journalist and humorist **George Ade**
[1866–1944], 'The Steel Box', in the Chicago Record,
16 March 1898

Education is going to college to learn to express your ignorance in scientific terms.

Anon

> *Gaudeamus igitur,*
> *Juvenes dum sumus:*
> *Post jocundam juventutem,*
> *Post molestam senectutem,*
> *Nos habebit humus.*
> **Anon**; *based on a medieval student song:*
> *'Let us then rejoice, / While we are young; / After the*
> *pleasures of youth, / After the burdens of old age, /*
> *Earth shall hold us'*

It takes most men five years to recover from a college education, and to learn that poetry is as vital to thinking as knowledge.

American essayist and critic **Brooks Justin Atkinson**
[1894–1984], 'August 31' in Once Around the Sun, 1951

A professor is one who talks in someone else's sleep.
Attributed to poet **W H Auden** *[1907–73]*

Universities incline wits to sophistry and affectation.
Courtier and philosopher **Francis Bacon** *[Lord Verulam, 1561–1626], Valerius Terminus of the Interpretation of Nature, 1603*

If a man is a fool, you don't train him out of being a fool by sending him to university. You merely turn him into a trained fool, ten times more dangerous.
Novelist **Desmond Bagley** *[1923–83]*

Most higher education is devoted to affirming the traditions and origins of an existing elite and transmitting them to new members.
American anthropologist and writer **Mary Catherine Bateson** *[b. 1939], Composing a Life, 1989*

I can't give you a brain, but I can give you a degree.
American author **L Frank Baum** *[1856–1919], The Wonderful Wizard of Oz, 1900, the Great Oz to the Scarecrow*

Undergraduates owe their happiness chiefly to the consciousness that they are no longer at school. The nonsense which was knocked out of them at school is all put gently back at Oxford or Cambridge.

Writer and caricaturist **Max Beerbohm** *[1872–1956],*
'Going Back to School', in More, 1899

Someone once said, Rumbold, that education is what is left when you have forgotten all you have ever learned. You appear to be trying to circumvent the process by learning as little as possible.

Playwright and actor **Alan Bennett** *[b. 1934],*
Forty Years On, 1969

Balkan Sobranies in a wooden box,
The college arms upon the lid; Tokay
And sherry in the cupboard; on the shelves
The University Statutes bound in blue,
Chrome Yellow, Prancing Bigger, Blunden, Keats.
Poet **John Betjeman** *[1906–84], Summoned by Bells, 1960*

Hard students are commonly troubled by gowts, catarrhes, rheums, cachexia, bradypepsia, bad eyes, stones and collick, crudities, oppilations, vertigo, winds, consumptions, and all such diseases as come by over much sitting; they are for the most part lean, dry, ill-coloured; spend their fortunes, lose their wits, and many times their lives; and all through immoderate pains and extraordinary studies.

Clergyman and writer **Robert Burton** *[1577–1640],*
The Anatomy of Melancholy, 1621

The true University of these days is a Collection of Books.

Scottish historian and philosopher **Thomas Carlyle**
[1795–1881], On Heroes, Hero Worship, and the Heroic
in History, 1841

Examinations are formidable even to the best prepared, for the greatest fool may ask more than the wisest man can answer.

Clergyman and writer **Charles Caleb Colton**
[1780–1832], Lacon, 1820

The average PhD thesis is nothing but the transference of bones from one graveyard to another.

American historian and folklorist **J Frank Dobie**
[1888–1964], A Texan in England, Chapter 1

The function of the university is not simply to teach bread-winning, or to furnish teachers for public schools or to be a center of polite society; it is, above all, to be the organ of that fine adjustment between real life and the growing knowledge of life, and adjustment which forms the secret of civilization.

American educationist and writer **W E B Du Bois**
[1868–1963], The Souls of Black Folk, 1903

The things taught in colleges and schools are not an education, but the means of education.

American poet and essayist **Ralph Waldo Emerson**
[1803–82], Journals, 1831

After Cambridge – unemployment,
No one wanted much to know.
Good degrees are good for nothing
In the business world below.
Poet **Gavin Ewart** *[1916–95], 'The Sentimental
Education'*

The competitive spirit is an ethos which it is the business
of universities ... to subdue and neutralise.
Actor and writer **Stephen Fry** *[b. 1957], Paperweight,
1992*

To the University of Oxford I acknowledge no
obligation; and she will as cheerfully renounce me for a
son, as I am willing to disclaim her for a mother. I spent
fourteen months at Magdalen College; they proved the
fourteen months the most idle and unprofitable of my
whole life.
Historian **Edward Gibbon** *[1737–94], Memoirs of
My Life and Writings, 1796*

The clever men at Oxford
Know all there is to be knowed.
But they none of them know one half as much
As intelligent Mr Toad!
Writer **Kenneth Grahame** *[1859–1932], The Wind in
the Willows, 1908*

You can lead a boy to college, but you cannot make him think.

American writer and editor **Elbert Hubbard**
[1856–1915]

Every man should have a college education in order to show him how little the thing is really worth.

American writer and editor **Elbert Hubbard**
[1856–1915]

Colleges are places where pebbles are polished and diamonds are dimmed.

American agnostic and lawyer **Robert G Ingersoll**
[1833–99], Prose-Poems and Selections, 1884

State a moral case to a ploughman and a professor. The former will decide it as well, and often better than the latter, because he has not been led astray by artificial rules.

US President **Thomas Jefferson** *[1743–1826], Papers of*
Thomas Jefferson, Volume 12, 1955

In a growing number of countries everyone has a qualified right to attend a university . . . The result is the emergence of huge caravanserais . . . where higher education is doled out rather like gruel in a soup kitchen.

Journalist and writer **Paul Johnson** *[b. 1928],*
The Spectator, 1996

Education is the inculcation of the incomprehensible into the indifferent by the incompetent.

> *Attributed to economist* **John Maynard Keynes**
> *[1883–1946]*

Universities hire professors the way some men choose wives – they want the ones the others will admire.

> *American professor of mathematics* **Morris Kline**
> *[1908–92], Why the Professor Can't Teach, 1972*

Rummidge . . . had lately suffered the mortifying fate of most English universities of its type (civic redbrick); having competed strenuously for fifty years with two universities chiefly valued for being old, it was, at the moment of drawing level, rudely overtaken in popularity and prestige by a batch of universities chiefly valued for being new.

> *Writer and playwright* **David Lodge** *[b. 1935],*
> *Changing Places, 1975*

The reason universities are so full of knowledge is that the students come with so much and they leave with so little.

> *Canadian writer* **Marshall McLuhan** *[1911–80],*
> *Antigonish Review, 1988*

It is tiresome to hear education discussed, tiresome to educate, and tiresome to be educated.

> *Whig Prime Minister* **Viscount Melbourne**
> *[William Lamb, 1779–1848]*

Once you have the cap and gown all you need to do is open your mouth. Whatever nonsense you talk becomes wisdom and all the rubbish, good sense.

French comic playwright **Molière** *[1622–73],*
in The Imaginary Invalid, Act 3, 1673

Like so many ageing college people, Pnin had long ceased to notice the existence of students on the campus.

Russian-born novelist **Vladimir Nabokov**
[1899–1977], Pnin, 1957

A university is an *alma mater*, knowing her children one by one, not a foundry or a mint, or a treadmill.

Attributed to cardinal and poet **John Henry Newman**
[1801–90]

A graduation ceremony is an event where the commencement speaker tells thousands of students dressed in identical caps and gowns that individuality is the key to success.

American comedian and speech-writer **Bob Orben**
[b. 1927]

It is the function of a liberal university not to give the right answers, but to ask right questions.

American writer **Cynthia Ozick** *[b. 1928], 'Women and*
Creativity', 1969

When Scythrop grew up, he was sent, as usual, to a public school, where a little learning was painfully beaten into him, and from thence to university, where it was carefully taken out of him; and he was sent home like a well-threshed ear of corn, with nothing in his head.

Novelist **Thomas Love Peacock** *[1785–1866],*
Nightmare Abbey, 1818

In examinations those who do not wish to know ask questions of those who cannot tell.

Lecturer and critic **Walter Raleigh** *[1861–1922],*
'Some Thoughts on Examinations', in Laughter from a
Cloud, 1923

A man who has never gone to school may steal from a freight car; but if he has a university education, he may steal the whole railroad.

US President **Theodore Roosevelt** *[1858–1919]*

Education is what survives when what has been learned has been forgotten.

American psychologist **B F Skinner** *[1904–90],*
New Scientist, 21 May 1964

Several of those learned societies have chosen to remain . . . the sanctuaries in which exploded systems and obsolete prejudices found shelter and protection, after they had been hunted out of every corner of the world.

Scottish Enlightenment economist and philosopher **Adam Smith** *[1723–90], Inquiry into the Nature and Causes of the Wealth of Nations, 1776*

Some men are graduated from college *cum laude*, some are graduated *summa cum laude*, and some are graduated *mirabile dictu*.

US President **William Howard Taft** *[1857–1930]*

Training is everything. The peach was once a bitter almond; cauliflower is nothing but cabbage with a college education.

American writer **Mark Twain** *[Samuel Langhorne Clemens, 1835–1910], 'Pudd'nhead Wilson's Calendar', Chapter 2, in Pudd'nhead Wilson, 1894*

So far as the mere imparting of information is concerned, no university has had any justification for existence since the popularization of printing in the fifteenth century.

Philosopher and mathematician **Alfred North Whitehead** *[1861–1947], The Aims of Education*

The exquisite art of idleness, one of the most important things that any university can teach.

Irish playwright and wit **Oscar Wilde** *[1854–1900]*

If a professor can be replaced by a CD-ROM, he or she should be.

American professor of management and president of Massachusetts University **Jack M Wilson** *[b. 1945]*

Bald heads forgetful of their sins,
Old, learned, respectable bald heads
Edit and annotate the lines
That young men, tossing on their beds,
Rhymed out in love's despair
To flatter beauty's ignorant ear.

All shuffle there; all cough in ink;
All wear the carpet with their shoes;
All think what other people think;
All know the man their neighbour knows.
Lord, what would they say
Did their Catullus walk that way?

Irish poet **William Butler Yeats** *[1865–1939], Catholic Anthology 1914–1915*

10
Men

Years ago, manhood was an opportunity for achievement, and now it is a problem to be overcome.

American writer **Garrison Keillor** *[b. 1942]*,
The Book of Guys, 1994

Poets galore have waxed lyrical about *man* down the centuries; but when it comes to *men*, it is a very different matter. For the last fifty years, men have been under attack, directly and indirectly – directly by feminist writers, indirectly by men themselves. Their former ineffable and effortless assumption of superiority has been crumbling inexorably under those sustained and insidious assaults. Men are getting a make-over; men are being forced – for the first time, perhaps – to see themselves as others see them; men have lost their empires and are still looking for a role. Poor things.

"

The first time Adam had a chance, he laid the blame on Eve.

Conservative politician **Nancy, Lady Astor**
[1879–1964]

There is less in this man than meets the eye.
American actress **Tallulah Bankhead** *[1903–68],*
commenting on a revival of Maeterlinck's play Aglavaine
and Selysette; in Alexander Woolcott, Shouts and
Murders

Man is the second strongest sex in the world.
American playwright **Philip Barry** *[1896–1949]*

Male, *n*: a member of the unconsidered, or negligible, sex. The male of the human species is commonly known to the female as Mere Man. The genus has two varieties: good providers and bad providers.
American journalist **Ambrose Bierce** *[1842–?1914],*
The Devil's Dictionary, 1906

Every modern male has, lying at the bottom of his psyche, a large, primitive being covered with hair down to his feet. Making contact with this Wild Man is the step the Eighties male or the Nineties male has yet to take.

American writer **Robert Bly** *[b. 1926], Iron John, 1990*

Men build bridges and throw railroads across deserts, and yet they contend successfully that the job of sewing on a button is beyond them. Accordingly, they don't have to sew buttons.

American journalist **Heywood Broun** *[1888–1939],
'Holding a Baby', Seeing Things at Night, 1921*

'Yes,' I answered you last night.
'No,' this morning, sir I say.
Colours seen by candle-light
Will not look the same by day.
Poet **Elizabeth Barrett Browning** *[1806–61]*

The male is a domestic animal which, if treated with firmness and kindness, can be trained to do most things.
Novelist **Jilly Cooper** *[b. 1942], in Cosmopolitan, 1972*

Bloody men are like bloody buses –
You wait for about a year
And as soon as one approaches your stop
Two or three others appear.
Poet **Wendy Cope** *[b. 1945], 'Bloody Men', 1992*

No man is a hero to his valet. – *Il n'y a point de héros pour son valet de chambre.*

French society hostess **Madame Cornuel**
[1605–94]

Men are what their mothers made them.
> *American poet and essayist* **Ralph Waldo Emerson**
> *[1803–82], The Conduct of Life, 1860*

All men are equal – all men, that is to say, who possess umbrellas.
> *Novelist* **E M Forster** *[1879–1970], Howards End,*
> *Chapter 10, 1910*

Whatever they may be in public life, whatever their relations with men, in their relations with women, all men are rapists, and that's all they are. They rape us with their eyes, their laws, and their codes.
> *America feminist writer* **Marilyn French** *[b. 1929],*
> *The Women's Room, 1977*

In the 19th century the problem was that *God is dead*; in the 20th century the problem is that *man is dead*. In the 19th century inhumanity meant cruelty; in the 20th century it means schizoid self-alienation. The danger of the past was that men became slaves. The danger of the future is that men may become robots.
> *American philosopher and psychologist* **Erich Fromm**
> *[1900–80], The Sane Society, 1955*

I want a man who's kind and understanding – is that too much to ask of a millionaire?
> *Hungarian film actress* **Zsa Zsa Gabor** *[b. c. 1919]*

Macho does not prove mucho.
Hungarian film actress **Zsa Zsa Gabor** *[b. c. 1919]*

A man . . . is *so* in the way in the house!
Novelist **Elizabeth Gaskell** *[1810–65], Cranford,*
Chapter 1, 1853

Women have very little idea of how much men hate
them.
Australian feminist writer and academic **Germaine**
Greer *[b. 1939], The Female Eunuch, 1971*

Behind every successful man stand a proud wife and a
surprised mother-in-law.
American Congressman **Lawrence Brooks Hays**
[1898–1981]

Can you imagine a world without men? No crime and
lots of happy fat women.
American cartoonist **Nicole Hollander**
['Sylvia', b. 1939]

Boys will be boys, and so will a lot of middle-aged men.
American humorist **Kin Hubbard** *[1868–1930]*

Men are very queer animals – a mixture of horse-
nervousness, ass-stubbornness and camel-malice.
Scientist **Thomas Henry Huxley** *[1825–95]*

No man is ever old enough to know better.
Journalist and editor **Holbrook Jackson** *[1874–1948],*
Ladies' Home Journal, January 1950

Beware of the man who praises Women's Liberation: he
is about to quit his job.
American writer **Erica Jong** *[b. 1942]*

Why can't a woman be more like a man?
Men are so honest, so thoroughly square;
Eternally noble, historically fair;
Who when you win, always give your back a pat.
Why can't a woman be like that?
American songwriter and playwright **Alan Jay Lerner**
[1918–86], 'A Hymn to Him', My Fair Lady, 1956

Man does not control his own fate. The women in his
life do that for him.
American comedian **Groucho Marx** *[1895–1977]*

Men have an extraordinarily erroneous opinion of their
position in nature; and the error is ineradicable.
Novelist and short-story writer **W Somerset Maugham**
[1874–1965], A Writer's Notebook, 1949

There is nothing about which men lie so much as about
their sexual powers. In this at least every man is, what in
his heart he would most like to be, a Casanova.
Novelist and short-story writer **W Somerset Maugham**
[1874–1965], A Writer's Notebook, 1949

Women want mediocre men, and men are working hard to be as mediocre as possible.

American anthropologist **Margaret Mead** *[1901–78],*
in Quote magazine, 15 June 1952

Women's Liberation is just a lot of foolishness. It's the men who are discriminated against. They can't bear children. And no one is likely to do anything about that.

Israeli Prime Minister **Golda Meir** *[1898–1978],*
Newsweek, 23 October 1972

Men have a much better time of it than women. For one thing, they marry later. For another thing, they die earlier.

American journalist and literary critic **H L Mencken**
[1880–1956], Chrestomathy, 1949

If men liked shopping, they'd call it research.

American singer and musician **Cynthia Nelms**
[1942–95]

Women and small men are hard to handle.

Proverb – *Chinese*

The follies which a man regrets most in his life are those which he didn't commit when he had the opportunity.

Anglo-American writer **Helen Rowland** *[1875–1950],*
A Guide to Men, 1922

Men who are unhappy, like men who sleep badly, are always proud of the fact.

> *Philosopher and mathematician* **Bertrand Russell**
> *[1872–1970], Conquest of Happiness, 1930*

I like men to behave like men. I like them strong and childish.

> *French writer* **Françoise Sagan** *[b. 1935]*

Men have more problems than women. In the first place, they have to put up with women.

> *French writer* **Françoise Sagan** *[b. 1935]*

Men hate to be misunderstood, and to be understood makes them furious.

> *American novelist* **Edgar Saltus** *[1855–1921]*

The more I see of men, the more I like dogs.

> *French woman of letters* **Madame de Stael**
> *[1766–1817]*

I know this – a man got to do what he got to do.

> *American novelist* **John Steinbeck** *[1902–68],*
> *The Grapes of Wrath, 1939*

However we brave it out, we men are a little breed.

> *Poet* **Alfred, Lord Tennyson** *[1809–92],*
> *in 'Maud'*

God created man because he was disappointed in the monkey.

American writer **Mark Twain** *[Samuel Langhorne Clemens, 1835–1910]*

You men are unaccountable things; mad till you have your mistresses, and then stark mad till you are rid of 'em again.

Architect and playwright **John Vanbrugh** *[1664–1726], The Provoked Wife, 1697*

A man in the house is worth two in the street.

American vaudeville and film actress **Mae West** *[1893–1980], Belle of the Nineties, 1934 film*

Give a man a free hand and he'll try to put it all over you.

American vaudeville and film actress **Mae West** *[1893–1980], Klondyke Annie, 1936 film*

It is easier for a man to be loyal to his club than to his planet; the by-laws are shorter, and he is personally acquainted with the other members.

Novelist **E B White** *[1899–1985]*

There is something positively brutal about the good nature of most modern men.

Irish playwright and wit **Oscar Wilde** *[1854–1900], A Woman of No Importance, 1893*

The only time a woman really succeeds in changing a man is when he's a baby.

American film actress **Natalie Wood** *[1938–81]*

11

Women

Never underestimate a man's ability to underestimate a woman. (Anon)

This is where I put my head on the block – again. In one of my guest stints in the Dictionary Corner of my favourite afternoon TV programme, *Countdown*, I ventured to offer a few quotations on, *inter alia*, women. The reactions of the studio audience were disconcerting: a few titters, yes; a few muted cheers, yes; but what took me aback was an outbreak of booing at one stage – polite booing, to be sure (this was *Countdown*, after all!), but booing nonetheless. It demonstrated very clearly what a treacherous minefield the war between the sexes still is. Perhaps I should not have been surprised. For centuries, all the way back to the Ancients of classical Greece and Rome, male writers have been dyed-in-the-wool misogynists, or have expressed dyed-

in-the-wool misogynist sentiments. Women have been merci-
lessly mocked or, much worse, patronised by men – and by some
women, too. The post-war feminist movement created totally
new rules of battle engagement; the scars have clearly not healed
yet. But please don't shoot the messenger!

66 99

The woman that deliberates is lost.
Essayist and politician **Joseph Addison** *[1672–1719],*
Cato, Act 4, Scene 1, 1713

Girls are so queer you never know what they mean. They
say No when they mean Yes, and drive a man out of his
wits for the fun of it . . .
American writer **Louisa May Alcott** *[1832–88], Little*
Women, 1869

Forgetting is woman's first and greatest art.
Novelist, poet and biographer **Richard Aldington**
[1892–1962], The Colonel's Daughter, 1931

It's the fallen women who are usually picked up.
American film director and actor **Woody Allen** *[b. 1937]*

Women are really much nicer than men:
No wonder we like them.
Novelist **Kingsley Amis** *[1922–95], 'A Bookshop Idyll',*
1956

A woman who is smart enough to ask a man's advice is seldom dumb enough to take it.

Anon

Woman was made after man, and man has been after her ever since.

Anon

He tries to get off with women because he cannot get on with them.

Anon

Beware of loose women in tight skirts and tight women in loose skirts.

Anon

With women the heart argues, not the mind.
Poet and essayist **Matthew Arnold** *[1822–88], Merope, 1858*

A woman especially, if she have the misfortune of knowing any thing, should conceal it as well as she can.
Novelist **Jane Austen** *[1775–1817], Northanger Abbey, published in 1818*

Some women . . . enjoy tremendously being told they look a mess – and they actually thrill to the threat of physical violence. I've never met one that does, mind you, but they probably do exist. In books. By men.

Playwright **Alan Ayckbourn** *[b. 1939],*
Round and Round the Garden, 1975

A woman can be anything that the man who loves her would have her be.

Scottish playwright **J M Barrie** *[1860–1937],*
Tommy and Grizel, 1900

One is not born a woman: one becomes a woman.

French novelist and feminist **Simone de Beauvoir**
[1908–86], The Second Sex, 1949

Most women are not so young as they are painted.

Writer and caricaturist **Max Beerbohm** *[1872–1956],*
Yellow Book, 1894

One of the few lessons I have learned in life is that there is invariably something odd about women who wear ankle socks.

Playwright and actor **Alan Bennett** *[b. 1934],*
Old Country, Act 1, 1978

Women should have labels on their foreheads saying, 'Government Health Warning: woman can seriously damage your brains, genitals, current account,

117

confidence, razor blades, and good standing among your friends'.

Journalist **Jeffrey Bernard** *[1932–97]*

Who can find a virtuous woman? For her price is far above rubies.

Bible, *Proverbs 31:10*

Here's to woman! Would that we could fall into her arms without falling into her hands.

American journalist **Ambrose Bierce** *[1842–?1914],*
cited in C H Grattan, Bitter Bierce, 1929

Behind almost every woman you ever heard of stands a man who let her down.

American writer and critic **Naomi Bliven**
[1916–2002]

I have reached the age when a woman begins to perceive that she is growing into the person she least plans to resemble: her mother.

Novelist and art historian **Anita Brookner** *[b. 1938],*
Incidents in the Rue Laugier, 1995

A woman's always younger than a man of equal years.

Poet **Elizabeth Barrett Browning** *[1806–61],*
'Aurora Leigh'

Auld nature swears, the lovely dears
Her noblest work she classes, O;
Her prentice han' she try'd on man,
An' then she made the lasses, O.
Scottish poet **Robert Burns** *[1759–96], 'Green Grow the
Rashes', 1783*

I heard a man say that brigands demand your money or
your life, whereas women require both.
Writer **Samuel Butler** *[1835–1902], Further Extracts
from Notebooks, 1934*

It was a blonde. A blonde to make a bishop kick a hole
in a stained glass window.
American detective fiction writer **Raymond Chandler**
[1888–1959], Farewell My Lovely, 1940

She opened her mouth like a fire bucket and laughed.
That terminated my interest in her. I couldn't hear the
laugh but the hole in her face when she unzipped her
teeth was all I needed.
American detective fiction writer **Raymond Chandler**
[1888–1959], The Long Goodbye

And what is better than wisedoome? Womman.
And what is better than a good womman? Nothyng.
Poet **Geoffrey Chaucer** *[c. 1345–1400], The Canterbury
Tales, 'The Tale of Melibee'*

Heaven has no Rage, like Love to Hatred turned,
Nor Hell a Fury, like a Woman scorn'd.

Playwright **William Congreve** *[1670–1729],*
The Mourning Bride, Act 3, 1697

A woman's desire for revenge outlasts all her other emotions.

Writer and critic **Cyril Connolly** *[1903–74],*
The Unquiet Grave, 1945

Being a woman is a terribly difficult task, since it consists principally in dealing with men.

Polish-born English novelist **Joseph Conrad**
[1857–1924]

Amanda: I've been brought up to believe that it's beyond the pale for a man to strike a woman.
Elyot: A very poor tradition. Certain women should be struck regularly, like gongs.

Writer and entertainer **Noël Coward** *[1899–1973],*
Private Lives, 1930

What is woman? – only one of Nature's agreeable blunders.

Playwright and poet **Hannah Cowley** *['Anna Matilda',*
1743–1809], Who's the Dupe?, 1779

Women never have young minds. They are born three thousand years old.

Playwright **Shelagh Delaney** *[b. 1939],*
A Taste of Honey, 1959

Most women set out to try to change a man, and when they have changed him they do not like him.

Attributed to German-born American actress and cabaret performer **Marlene Dietrich** *[1901–92]*

The entire being of a woman is a secret which should be kept.

Danish writer **Isak Dinesen** *[Karen Blixen, 1885–1962], 'Of Hidden Thoughts and of Heaven', Last Tales, 1957*

I'm not denyin' the women are foolish; God Almighty made 'em to match the men.

Novelist **George Eliot** *[Mary Ann Evans, 1819–80], Adam Bede, 1859*

A woman's strength is the unresistible might of weakness.

American poet and essayist **Ralph Waldo Emerson** *[1803–82], Journals, 1836*

When a woman behaves like a man, why doesn't she behave like a nice man?

Actress **Edith Evans** *[1888–1976]*

No woman can be a beauty without a fortune.

Irish playwright **George Farquhar** *[1678–1707], The Beaux' Stratagem, 1707*

The great question that has never been answered and which I have not yet been able to answer, despite my thirty years of research into the feminine soul, is 'What does a woman want?'

Austrian psychoanalyst **Sigmund Freud** *[1856–1939], in a letter to Marie Bonaparte, quoted in Ernest Jones, Sigmund Freud: Life and Work, 1955*

The stereotype is the Eternal Feminine. She is the Sexual Object sought by all men, and by all women. She is of neither sex, for she has herself no sex at all. Her value is solely attested by the demand she excites in others. All she must contribute is her existence. She need achieve nothing, for she is the reward of achievement.

Australian feminist writer and academic **Germaine Greer** *[b. 1939], The Female Eunuch, 1970*

A woman's mind is cleaner than a man's. She changes it more often.

American writer **Oliver Herford** *[1863–1935]*

Man has his will – but woman has her way.

American physician and writer **Oliver Wendell Holmes, Sr** *[1809–94], The Autocrat of the Breakfast Table, Chapter 12, 1857–8*

A woman is as old as she looks before breakfast.

American humorist **Edgar Watson Howe** *[1853–1937], Country Town Sayings, 1911*

Woman's intuition is the result of millions of years of not thinking.

American author **Rupert Hughes** *[1872–1956]*

There is in every true woman's heart a spark of heavenly fire, which lies dormant in the broad daylight of prosperity, but which kindles up and beams and blazes in the dark hour of adversity.

American writer **Washington Irving** *[1783–1859],*
'The Broken Heart', The Sketch Book of Geoffrey Crayon,
Gent., 1819–20

Sir, a woman's preaching is like a dog's walking on his hinder legs. It is not done well; but you are surprised to find it done at all.

Writer and lexicographer **Samuel Johnson**, *in Boswell's*
Life of Johnson, Volume 1, 31 July 1763

The great trick with a woman is to get rid of her while she thinks she's getting rid of you.

Danish philosopher **Sören Kierkegaard** *[1813–55]*

And a woman is only a woman,
but a good Cigar is a Smoke.

Poet and novelist **Rudyard Kipling** *[1865–1936],*
'The Betrothed', 1886

. . . For the female of the species is more deadly than the male.

Poet and novelist **Rudyard Kipling** *[1865–1936],*
'The Female of the Species', 1911

To promote a Woman to bear rule, superiority, dominion or empire, above any Realm, Nation, or City, is repugnant to Nature; contumely to God, a thing most contrarious to his revealed will and approved ordinance; and finally it is the subversion of good Order, of all equity and justice . . . Nature, I say, doth paint them further to be weak, frail, impatient, feeble, and foolish; and experience hath declared them to be unconstant, variable, cruel, and lacking the spirit of counsel and regiment.

Scottish Protestant Reformer **John Knox** *[c. 1513–72],*
First Blast of the Trumpet Against the Monstrous
Regiment of Women, 1558

Thank heaven for little girls!
For little girls get bigger every day.
American songwriter **Alan Jay Lerner** *[1918–86],*
'Thank Heaven for Little Girls', 1958

She's the sort of woman who lives for others – you can always tell the others by their hunted expression.

Scholar and religious writer **C S Lewis** *[1898–1963],*
The Screwtape Letters, 1942

God created Adam lord of all living creatures, but Eve spoiled it all.

German religious reformer **Martin Luther** *[1483–1546]*

Our bodies are shaped to bear children, and our lives are a working-out of the processes of creation. All our ambitions and intelligence are beside that great elemental point.

American poet and writer **Phyllis McGinley** *[1905–78], 'The Honor of Being a Woman', The Province of the Heart, 1959*

Women do not find it difficult nowadays to behave like men; but they often find it extremely difficult to behave like gentlemen.

Scottish writer **Compton Mackenzie** *[1883–1972], Literature in My Time, 1933*

Arguing with a woman is like trying to fold the airmail edition of *The Times* in a high wind.

Author **Lord Mancroft** *[1917–87]*

A woman will always sacrifice herself if you give her the opportunity. It is her favourite form of self-indulgence.

Novelist and short-story writer **W Somerset Maugham** *[1874–1965], The Circle, Chapter 3, 1921*

A misogynist is a man who hates women as much as women hate each other.

American journalist and literary critic **H L Mencken** *[1880–1956]*

I expect that woman will be the last thing civilised by man.

> *Novelist and poet* **George Meredith** *[1828–1909],*
> *The Ordeal of Richard Feverel, 1859*

O why did God,
Creator wise, that peopl'd highest Heav'n
With Spirits Masculine, create at last
This noveltie on Earth, this fair defect
Of Nature?
Poet **John Milton** *[1608–74], Paradise Lost, 1667*

A woman should shed her modesty with her clothes and recover it when she puts them on again.

> *French essayist* **Michel de Montaigne** *[1533–92]*

American Women: How they mortify the flesh in order to make it appetising! Their beauty is a vast industry, their enduring allure a discipline which nuns or athletes might find excessive.

> *Writer and broadcaster* **Malcolm Muggeridge**
> *[1903–90], 'Women of America', The Most of Malcolm*
> *Muggeridge, 1966*

Women would rather be right than be reasonable.

> *American poet* **Ogden Nash** *[1902–71],*
> *'Frailty, Thy Name Is a Misnomer',*
> *Marriage Lines, 1964*

Oh woman! Lovely woman! Nature made thee
To temper man: we had been brutes without you;
Angels are painted fair, to look like you;
Here's in you all that we believe of heav'n,
Amazing brightness, purity, and truth,
Eternal joy, and everlasting love.

Playwright **Thomas Otway** *[1652–85], Venice Preserv'd,*
1682

Nature intended women to be our slaves . . . they are
our property; we are not theirs. They belong to us, just
as a tree that bears fruit belongs to a gardener. What a
mad idea to demand equality for women! . . . Women
are nothing but machines for producing children.

French emperor **Napoleon I** *[1769–1821]*

After equality and wage parity and liberation of body
and soul, women still can't do the following: start
barbecue fires; hook up a stereo; shine shoes; decide
where to hang a picture; investigate mysterious house
noises at night; kill and dispose of large insects; walk
past a mirror without stopping to look.

American humorist **P J O'Rourke** *[b. 1947]*

Slamming their doors, stamping their high heels,
banging their irons and saucepans – the eternal flaming
racket of the female.

Playwright **John Osborne** *[1929–94],*
Look Back in Anger, 1956

If civilization had been left in female hands, we would still be living in grass huts.

American author and critic **Camille Paglia** *[b. 1947],*
Sexual Personae, 1990

We are here to claim our right as women, not only to be free, but to fight for freedom. That is our right as well as our duty.

Suffragette **Christabel Pankhurst** *[1880–1958],*
speech in London, 23 March 1911

Regret is a woman's natural food – she thrives upon it.

Playwright **Arthur Wing Pinero** *[1855–1934],*
Sweet Lavender, 1888

Women are quite unlike men. Women have higher voices, longer hair, smaller waistlines, daintier feet and prettier hands. They also invariably have the upper hand.

Humorist **Stephen Potter** *[1900–69], advertisement for*
Ladies' Home Journal, 17 September 1957

All are good maids, but whence come the bad wives?

Proverb – *English*

God sent us women and the devil sent them corsets.

Proverb – *French*

A woman prefers a man without money to money without a man.

Proverb – *Greek*

Women and calendars are good only for a year.

Proverb – *Spanish*

A woman is like a teabag – you can't tell how strong she is until you put her in hot water.

Attributed to former US First Lady **Nancy Reagan**
[b. 1921]

I consider that women who are authors, lawyers and politicians are monsters.

French impressionist painter **Pierre Auguste Renoir**
[1840–1919]

I believe in women. Men are just unsubstantiated rumors.

Canadian playwright **Erika Ritter** *[b. 1948]*

I think that business practices would improve immeasurably if they were guided by 'feminine' principles and qualities like love and care and intuition.

Businesswoman **Anita Roddick** *[b. 1942]*,
Body and Soul, 1991

Women and elephants never forget an injury.

Scottish writer **Saki** *[H H Munro, 1870–1916]*,
'Reginald on Besetting Sins', Reginald, 1904

Do you not know I am a woman? When I think, I must speak.

Playwright **William Shakespeare** *[1564–1616]*,
As You Like It, Act 3, Scene 2, Rosalind to Celia, 1504

Frailty, thy name is woman!
Playwright **William Shakespeare** *[1564–1616], Hamlet,*
Act 1, Scene 2, Hamlet about his mother Gertrude

The lady doth protest too much, methinks.
Playwright **William Shakespeare** *[1564–1616], Hamlet,*
Act 3, Scene 2, Gertrude, about the queen in the
play-within-the-play, The Mouse-trap

She's as headstrong as an allegory on the banks of the Nile.
Irish dramatist and politician **Richard Brinsley**
Sheridan *[1751–1816], The Rivals, Act 3, Scene 1,*
Mrs Malaprop speaking

Literature cannot be the business of a woman's life.
Poet **Robert Southey** *[1774–1843], in a letter to*
Charlotte Brontë

A woman seldom writes her mind but in her postscript.
Irish-born essayist **Richard Steele** *[1672–1729],*
in the Spectator, 31 May 1711

A woman without a man is like a fish without a bicycle.
Attributed to American feminist writer **Gloria Steinem**
[b. 1934]

Women are stronger than men – they do not die of wisdom.
They are better than men because they do not seek wisdom.
They are wiser than men because they know less and
understand more.

Irish poet and writer **James Stephens** *[1882–1950],*
The Crock of Gold, Book 1, 1912

It is clearly absurd that it should be possible for a woman
to qualify as a saint with direct access to the Almighty
when she may not qualify as a curate.

Feminist crusader **Mary Stocks** *[1891–1975]*

The penalty for getting the woman you want is that you
must keep her.

Biographer and critic **Lytton Strachey**
[1880–1932]

A very little wit is valued in a woman, as we are pleased
at the few words of a parrot.

Anglo-Irish writer and clergyman **Jonathan Swift**
[1667–1745]

A woman's place is in the wrong.

American cartoonist and writer **James Thurber**
[1894–1961]

Feminism is the most revolutionary idea there has ever been. Equality for women demands a change in the human psyche more profound than anything Marx dreamed of. It means valuing parenthood as much as we value banking.

Journalist **Polly Toynbee** *[b. 1956], The Guardian, 19 January 1987*

From birth to 18 a girls needs good parents. From 18 to 35, she needs good looks. From 35 to 55, good personality. From 55 on, she needs good cash.

American vaudeville artiste **Sophie Tucker** *[1884–1966], quoted in Michael Freedland, Sophie, 1978*

Once a woman has given you her heart you can never get rid of the rest of her.

Architect and playwright **John Vanbrugh** *[1664–1726], The Relapse, 1696*

When women go wrong, men go right after them.

American vaudeville and film actress **Mae West** *[1893–1980], in She Done Him Wrong, 1933 film*

Whatever women do they must do twice as well as men to be thought half as good. Luckily, this is not difficult.

Canadian writer and politician **Charlotte Whitton** *[1896–1975], in Canada Month, June 1963*

Women have a much better time than men in this world. There are far more things forbidden to them.

Irish playwright and wit **Oscar Wilde** *[1854–1900]*

Women are a decorative sex. They never have anything to say, but they say it charmingly.

Irish playwright and wit **Oscar Wilde** *[1854–1900],*
The Picture of Dorian Gray, 1891

No woman should ever be quite accurate about her age. It looks so calculating.

Irish playwright and wit **Oscar Wilde** *[1854–1900],*
The Importance of Being Earnest, 1895

If woman had no existence save in the fiction written by men, one would imagine her a person of the utmost importance; very various; heroic and mean; splendid and sordid; infinitely beautiful and hideous in the extreme; as great as a man, some think even greater.

Novelist **Virginia Woolf** *[1882–1941], A Room of One's*
Own, Chapter 3, 1929

12
Sex

Steady, Mabel, we're passing the club.
Caption for a cartoon by **Ronald Searle** *[b. 1920],*
of a city gent and his floosie in the back of a taxi

It is such a fascinating subject – sex. Some people may 'not care
a biscuit for it' (see T E Lawrence, *below*). Others seem to
be obsessed with it (see Woody Allen, *below*). Most people,
however, surely have a healthy interest in the subject, in their
ordinary lives, in their secret lives or in their fantasies; from
adolescence to old age it can dominate one's thinking and
actions. In this section I have chosen to separate 'sex' from 'love'
(*see next section*), but the distinction is a blurred and, you may
think, an unreal one. Take your pick.

"

Sex without love is an empty experience, but as empty experiences go, it's a pretty good empty experience.
American film actor and writer **Woody Allen** *[b. 1937]*

Is sex dirty? Only if it's done right.
American film actor and writer **Woody Allen** *[b. 1937],*
Everything You Always Wanted to Know About Sex, 1972
film

After coition, every animal is sad.

Anon

Give me chastity and continence – but not yet.
Christian theologian and saint **Augustine of Hippo**
[354–430], Confessions, 397–98

My mother used to say, Delia, if S-E-X ever rears its ugly head, close your eyes before you see the rest of it.
Playwright **Alan Ayckbourn** *[b. 1939], Bedroom Farce,*
Act 2, 1978

Norman doesn't bother with secret signals. It was just wham, thump and there we were on the rug.
Playwright **Alan Ayckbourn** *[b. 1939], Table Manners,*
1975

Money, it turned out, was exactly like sex, you thought of nothing else if you didn't have it and thought of other things if you did.

American novelist **James Baldwin** *[1924–87],
in 'Black Boy Looks at the White Boy', Esquire, May 1961*

I'll come and make love to you at five o'clock. If I'm late, start without me.

American actress **Tallulah Bankhead** *[1903–68], quoted
in Ted Morgan, Somerset Maugham, 1980*

Sexuality is the lyricism of the masses.

French poet **Charles Beaudelaire** *[1821–67], Intimate
Journals, translated by Christopher Isherwood, 1887*

I've never yet turned over a fig leaf that didn't have a price tag on the other side.

Canadian-born novelist **Saul Bellow** *[b. 1915]*

Embraces are comminglings: from the Head even to
  the Feet;
And not a pompous High Priest entering by a secret
  place.

Poet and painter **William Blake** *[1757–1827]*

When you're getting it you don't think about it, and when you aren't getting it you think of nothing but.

Novelist **Celia Brayfield** *[b. 1945], interview in the
Evening Standard, c. 1975*

136

I could be content that we might procreate like trees, without conjunction, or that there were any way to perpetuate the World without this trivial and vulgar way of coition: it is the foolishest act a wise man commits in all his life; nor is there any thing that will more deject his cool'd imagination, when he shall consider what an odd and unworthy piece of folly he hath committed.

Author and physician **Sir Thomas Browne** *[1605–82],*
Religio Medici, 1643

Sex, on the whole, was meant to be short, nasty and brutish. If what you want is cuddling, you should buy a puppy.

Journalist **Julie Burchill** *[b. 1960], Sex and Sensibility,*
1992

He said it was artificial respiration, but now I find I am to have his child.

Novelist **Anthony Burgess** *[1917–93],*
Inside Mr Enderby, 1963

There's nothing wrong with making love with the light on. Just make sure the car door is closed.

American comedian **George Burns** *[1896–1996]*

I would read *Playboy* magazine more often, but my glasses keep steaming over.

American comedian **George Burns** *[1896–1996]*

(She did all this like a good girl), and I took the opportunity of some dry horse-litter, and gave her such a thundering scalade that electrified the very marrow of her bones.

*Scottish poet **Robert Burns** [1759–96], describing his reunion with the pregnant Jean Armour in a letter to his friend, Robert Ainslie, in February 1788; shortly afterwards Jean give birth to twin girls, both of whom died within a few days*

What men call gallantry, and gods adultery,
Is much more common where the climate's sultry.
*Poet **George Lord Byron** [1788–1824], Don Juan, 1819–24*

It doesn't matter what you do in the bedroom as long as you don't do it in the street and frighten the horses.

*Actress **Mrs Patrick Campbell** [Beatrice Stella Tanner, 1865–1940], on homosexuality: quoted in Daphne Fielding's The Duchess of Jermyn Street, 1964*

Sexual intercourse is a grossly overrated pastime: the position is undignified, the pleasure momentary and the consequences utterly damnable.

*Dubiously attributed to politician and writer **Lord Chesterfield** [1694–1773]; an alternative version reads: 'The pleasure is momentary, the position ridiculous and the expense damnable.'*

Do not adultery commit;
Advantage rarely comes of it.
Poet **Arthur Hugh Clough** *[1819–61],*
'The Latest Decalogue', 1862

If our elaborate and dominating bodies are given us to
be denied at every turn, if our nature is always wrong
and wicked, how ineffectual we are – like fishes not
meant to swim.
Writer and critic **Cyril Connolly** *[1903–74],*
The Unquiet Grave, 1945

Sex is the great amateur art. The professional, male or
female, is frowned on; he or she misses the whole point
and spoils the show.
American editor and writer **David Cort** *[b. 1904],*
Social Astonishments, 1963

To me the whole business is vastly overrated. I enjoy it
for what it is worth and intend to go on doing so for as
long as anybody's interested, and when the time comes
that they are not I shall be perfectly content to settle
down with an apple and a good book.
Writer and entertainer **Noël Coward** *[1899–1973],*
Present Laughter, spoken by the actor-manager
Garry Esendine

I became one of the stately homos of England.
Writer **Quentin Crisp** *[1908–99],*
The Naked Civil Servant, 1968

What most men desire is a virgin who is a whore.
American novelist and critic **Edward Dahlberg**
[1900–77], 'On Lust', in Affairs of the Heart, 1965

My wife is a sex object: every time I ask for sex, she objects.
Comedian **Les Dawson** *[1934–93]*

A terrible thing happened to me again last night – nothing.
American comedienne **Phyllis Diller** *[1917–74]*

License my roving hands, and let them go,
Before, behind, between, above, below.
O my America, my new-found-land,
My kingdom, safeliest when with one man mann'd.
Poet and divine **John Donne** *[1572–1631], 'To His
Mistress Going to Bed', 1595*

Sex exists on both sides of the law, but the law itself creates the sides.
American feminist and writer **Andrea Dworkin**
[b. 1946], Intercourse, 1987

Seduction is often difficult to distinguish from rape. In seduction, the rapist bothers to buy a bottle of wine . . .
American feminist and writer **Andrea Dworkin**
[b. 1946], Letters from a War Zone, 1988

The sexual embrace can only be compared with music and with prayer.

> *Physician and writer* **Havelock Ellis** *[1859–1939],*
> *On Life and Sex: Essays of Love and Virtue, 1937*

Women need a reason to have sex. Men need a place.

> *American writer and journalist* **Nora Ephron** *[b. 1941],*
> *When Harry Met Sally, 1989 film*

Sex is a human activity like any other. It's a natural urge, like breathing, thinking, drinking, laughing, talking with friends, golf. They are not crimes if you plan them with someone other than your wife. Why should sex be?

> *Scottish lawyer and politician* **Nicholas Fairbairn**
> *[1933–95], in the Independent, 1992*

He in a few minutes ravished this fair creature, or at least would have ravished her, if she had not, by a timely compliance, prevented him.

> *Novelist and judge* **Henry Fielding** *[1707–54],*
> *Jonathan Wild, 1743*

A walk, a smile, a gait, a way of flicking the hair away from the eyes, the manner in which clothes encase the body, these can be erotic, but I would be greatly in the debt of the man who could tell me what could ever be appealing about those damp, dark, foul-smelling and revoltingly tufted areas of the body that constitute the main dishes in the banquet of love.

> *Writer and actor* **Stephen Fry** *[b. 1957], Paperweight, 1992*

I know nothing about sex because I was always married.
Hungarian-born film actress **Zsa Zsa Gabor** *[b. c. 1919]*

Prostitution gives her an opportunity to meet people. It provides fresh air and wholesome exercise, and it keeps her out of trouble.
American novelist **Joseph Heller** *[1923–99],*
Catch-22, 1961

People will insist on treating the *mons Veneris* as though it were Mount Everest.
Novelist and writer **Aldous Huxley** *[1894–1963],*
Eyeless in Gaza, 1936

The trees along the banks of the Royal Canal are more sinned against than sinning.
Irish poet **Patrick Kavanagh** *[1904–67]*

Being kissed by a man who *didn't* wax his moustache was – like eating an egg without salt.
Writer **Rudyard Kipling** *[1865–1936], 'Poor Dear*
Mamma', in The Story of the Gadsbys, 1889

> Sexual intercourse began
> In nineteen sixty three
> (Which was rather late for me)
> Between the end of the *Chatterley* ban
> And the Beatles' first LP.

Poet **Philip Larkin** *[1932–85], 'Annus Mirabilis', 1974*

Surely the sex business isn't worth all this damned fuss? I've met only a handful of people who cared a biscuit for it.

Writer **T E Lawrence** *[1888–1935] on reading*
Lady Chatterley's Lover, quoted in Christopher Hassall,
Edward Marsh, 1959

There is no bigger fan of the opposite sex than me, and I have the bills to prove it.

American songwriter and playwright **Alan J Lerner**
[1918–86]

A Jewish nymphomaniac is a woman who will make love with a man the same day she has had her hair done.

Actress and writer **Maureen Lipman** *[b. 1946]*

A promiscuous person is someone who is getting more sex than you are.

Publishing executive **Victor Lownes** *[b. 1928],*
in Playboy magazine

A nymphomaniac is a woman as obsessed with sex as the average man.

American journalist and author **Mignon McLaughlin**
[b. 1915]

To the mind of the modern girl, legs, like busts, are power points which she has been taught to tailor, but as parts of the success kits rather than erotically or sensuously.

Canadian writer **Marshall McLuhan** *[1911–80],*
The Mechanical Bride, 1951

Barnardine: Thou hast committed –
Barabas: Fornication? But that was in another country:
And besides, the wench is dead.
> *Playwright* **Christopher Marlowe** *[1564–93],*
> *The Jew of Malta, c. 1592*

If sex is such a natural phenomenon, how come there are
so many books on how to?
> *American singer and actress* **Bette Midler** *[b. 1944]*

Continental people have a sex life; the English have hot-
water bottles.
> *Hungarian-born writer* **George Mikes** *[1912–87],*
> *How to be an Alien, 1946*

I wanted to be a sex maniac but I failed the practical.
> *American film actor* **Robert Mitchum** *[1917–97]*

Louisa says, once you get used to it, it's utter utter utter
blissikins.
> *Writer* **Nancy Mitford** *[1904–73], Love in a Cold*
> *Climate, Chapter 11, 1949: Victoria talking to her*
> *cousins about IT*

I still enjoy sex at 71. I live at Number 73, so it's not too
far to walk.
> *Comedian* **Bob Monkhouse** *[1928–2003]*

I am always looking for meaningful one-night stands.
> *Actor* **Dudley Moore** *[1935–2002]*

The orgasm has replaced the Cross as the focus of longing and the image of fulfilment.

Writer and broadcaster **Malcolm Muggeridge**
[1903–90], 'Down With Sex', in The Most of Malcolm
Muggeridge, 1966

An orgy looks particularly alluring seen through the mists of righteous indignation.

Writer and broadcaster **Malcolm Muggeridge**
[1903–90], 'Dolce Vita in a Cold Climate', in The Most of
Malcolm Muggeridge, 1966

A girl who is bespectacled
Seldom gets her nectacled.

American poet **Ogden Nash** *[1902–71], Lines Written to*
Console Those Ladies by the Lines 'Men Seldom Make
Passes, etc', in Hard Lines, 1931

There are a number of mechanical devices which increase sexual arousal, particularly in women. Chief among these is the Mercedes-Benz 380SL convertible.

American humorous writer **P J O'Rourke** *[b. 1947]*

Dating is a social engagement with the threat of sex at its conclusion.

American humorous writer **P J O'Rourke** *[b. 1947],*
Modern Manners, 1984

Thank God we're normal,
Yes, this is our finest shower!
Playwright **John Osborne** *[1929–94], The Entertainer,*
1957

That woman speaks eighteen languages and she can't say 'No' in any of them.
American wit and journalist **Dorothy Parker** *[1893–1967]*

One more drink and I'd have been under the host.
American wit and journalist **Dorothy Parker**
[1893–1967]

Men seldom make passes
At girls who wear glasses.
American wit and journalist **Dorothy Parker**
[1893–1967], 'News Item'. Other alleged lines include
'You don't get sex / With specs' and 'No one ogles /
A girl in bi-fogles'.

I know it (sex) does make people happy, but to me it is just like having a cup of tea.
Brothel-keeper **Cynthia Payne** *('Madame Sin'), quoted in*
the Observer, 8 February 1987

Doing, a filthy pleasure is, and short;
And done, we straight repent us of the sport.
Let us not then rush blindly on unto it,
Like lustful beasts, that only know to do it:
For lust will languish, and that heat decay.

But thus, thus, keeping endless holiday,
Let us together closely lie, and kiss,
There is no labour, nor no shame in this;
This hath pleased, doth please, and long will please;
    never
Can this decay, but is beginning ever.

Roman satirist **Petronius Arbiter** *[d. AD 65],*
translated by Ben Jonson

You don't appreciate a lot of stuff in school until you get older. Little things like being spanked every day by a middle-aged woman – stuff you pay good money for in later life.

American comedian **Emo Philips** *[b. 1956]*

My classmates would copulate with anything that moved, but I never saw any reason to limit myself.

American comedian **Emo Philips** *[b. 1956]*

It's so long since I've had sex I've forgotten who ties up whom.

American comedienne **Joan Rivers** *[b. 1933]*

I blame my mother for my poor sex life. All she told me was, 'The man goes on top and the woman underneath.' For three years my husband and I slept in bunk beds.

American comedienne **Joan Rivers** *[b. 1933]*

I have so little sex appeal my gynaecologist calls me 'sir'.

American comedienne **Joan Rivers** *[b. 1933]*

It takes a lot of experience for a girl to kiss like a beginner.
American comedienne **Joan Rivers** *[b. 1933]*

Is it not strange that desire should so many years outlive performance?
Playwright **William Shakespeare** *[1564–1616],*
Henry IV, Part 2, Act 2, Scene 4, Poins, speaking about
Falstaff

I have made love to ten thousand women.
Belgian writer **Georges Simenon** *[1903–89], in*
L'Express, 2 February 1977; later, his second wife Denyse
amended the figure to 'no more than twelve hundred',
Sunday Times, 20 February 1983

How long do you want to wait until you start enjoying life? When you're sixty-five you get social security, not girls.
Playwright **Neil Simon** *[b. 1927], Come Play Your Horn,*
1961

What pornography is really about, ultimately, isn't sex but death.
American writer **Susan Sontag** *[b. 1933], in Partisan*
Review, December 1964

'Sex', she says, 'is a subject like any other subject. Every bit as interesting as agriculture.'
Scottish novelist **Muriel Spark** *[b. 1918]*

Traditionally, sex has been a very private, secretive activity. Herein perhaps lies its powerful force for uniting people in a strong bond. As we make sex less secretive, we may rob it of its power to hold men and women together.

Hungarian-born psychiatrist **Thomas Szasz** *[b. 1920],*
'Sex', The Second Sin, 1973

Chasing the naughty couples down the grassgreen gooseberried double bed of the wood.

Welsh poet and writer **Dylan Thomas** *[1914–53],*
Under Milk Wood, 1954

She said he proposed something on their wedding night that even her own brother wouldn't have suggested.

American cartoonist and writer **James Thurber**
[1894–1961]

Brains are never a handicap to a girl if she hides them under a see-through blouse.

American entertainer **Bobby Vinton** *[b. 1935]*

Reading about sex in yesterday's novels is liking watching people smoke in old films.

Novelist and scriptwriter **Fay Weldon** *[b. 1931],*
in the Guardian, 1 December 1989

149

In my day, I would only have sex with a man if I found him extremely attractive. These days, girls seem to choose them in much the same way as they might choose to suck on a boiled sweet.

Novelist **Mary Wesley** *[b. 1912], in the Independent, 18 October 1997*

It's not the men in my life that counts – it's the life in my men.

American vaudeville and film actress **Mae West** *[1893–1980], in I'm No Angel, 1933 film*

Ten men waiting for me at the door? Send one of them home, I'm tired.

American vaudeville and film actress **Mae West** *[1893–1980]*

Outside every thin woman is a fat man trying to get in.

Journalist **Katharine Whitehorn** *[b. 1928]*

13

Love and courtship

> Oh, what a dear ravishing thing is the beginning of an Amour!
>
> *English writer and adventuress* **Aphra Behn**
> *[1640–89], The Emperor of the Moon, 1687*

They love too much that die for love. All is fair in love and war. Love laughs at locksmiths. True love never grows cold. There's no love like the first love. Lucky at cards, unlucky in love – there is no end of proverbial saws about 'love'. Every person who ever put pen to paper seems to have had something to say about the subject of the love which makes the world go round. The problem for any anthologist is selection: I scribbled down scores of quotes in my youth, when the pangs of love caused such disruption to the act of living. Any selection tends to be a chronicle of what one was feeling and enduring at the time of dawning love, and then the resolution of love, through marriage or whatever. You don't have to be a poet to experience the poetry of love, the joy of love, the despair of love, the birth and death of love. You just have to be alive.

"99

Those marriages generally abound most with love and constancy that are preceded by a long courtship. The passion should strike root and gather strength before marriage be grafted on it.

Essayist and politician **Joseph Addison** *[1672–1719],*
Spectator, No. 261

Love is the answer, but while you're waiting for the answer, sex raises some pretty good questions.

American film actor and writer **Woody Allen** *[b. 1937],*
1975

The only thing you have to earn is love; all the rest you can steal.

Anon

A small love which warms is better than a great one which burns. – *Mieux vaut un petit amour qui chauffe qu'un grand qui brûle.*

Anon

A kiss which speaks volumes is rarely a first edition.

Anon

Western wind, when wilt thou blow,
The small rain down can rain?
Christ, if my love were in my arms
And I in my bed again!

Anon

Love is, above all, the gift of oneself.
French playwright **Jean Anouilh** *[1910–87],*
Ardèle ou la Marguerite, 1949

He was my North, my South, my East, my West,
My working week and my Sunday rest,
My noon, my midnight, my talk, my song;
I thought that love would last for ever. I was wrong.
Poet **W H Auden** *[1907–73], 'Funeral Blues',*
originally in the play The Ascent of F6, 1937

All the privilege I claim for my own sex . . . is that of
loving longest, when existence or when hope is gone.
Novelist **Jane Austen** *[1775–1817], Persuasion, 1818*

It is impossible to love and be wise.
Philosopher and politician **Francis Bacon** *[1561–1626],*
'Of Love', in Essays, 1625

Women are programmed to love completely, and men
are programmed to spread it around.
Novelist **Beryl Bainbridge** *[b. 1933], Daily Telegraph,*
10 September 1996

People in love, it is well known, suffer extreme conceptual delusions; the most common of those being that other people find your condition as thrilling and eye-watering as you do yourself.

Novelist **Julian Barnes** *[b. 1946]*

Love is the delightful interval between meeting a girl and discovering she looks like a haddock.

Attributed to American film actor **John Barrymore** *[1882–1942]*

Love ceases to be a pleasure when it ceases to be a secret.

English writer and adventuress **Aphra Behn** *[1640–89]*

Ten years of courtship is carrying celibacy to extremes.

Playwright and actor **Alan Bennett** *[b. 1934],* Habeas Corpus, *1973*

We sat in the car park till twenty to one
And now I'm engaged to Miss Joan Hunter Dunn.

Poet **John Betjeman** *[1906–84], 'A Subaltern's Love Song', 1945*

Charity (Love) suffereth long, and is kind; charity
envieth not; charity vaunteth not itself, is not puffed up,
Doth not behave itself unseemly, seeketh not her own,
is not easily provoked, thinketh no evil;
Rejoiceth not in iniquity, but rejoiceth in the truth;
Beareth all things, believeth all things, hopeth all
things, endureth all things;

Charity never faileth: but whether there be prophecies, they shall fail; whether there be tongues, they shall cease; whether there be knowledge, it shall vanish away.

Bible, *1 Corinthians 13:4–8*

And now abideth faith, hope, charity (love), these three; but the greatest of these is charity.

Bible, *1 Corinthians 13:13*

There is no fear in love; but perfect love casteth out fear.

Bible, *1 John 4:18*

Stay me with flagons, comfort me with apples: for I am sick of love.

Bible, *Song of Solomon 2:5*

Love, *n*: a temporary insanity curable by marriage or the removal of the patient from the influences under which he incurred the disease . . . It is sometimes fatal, but more frequently to the physician than to the patient.

American journalist **Ambrose Bierce** *[1842–?1914],*
The Devil's Dictionary, 1911

> Love seeketh not Itself to please,
> Nor for itself hath any care,
> But for another gives its ease,
> And builds a Heaven in Hell's despair.

Poet and painter **William Blake** *[1757–1827], 'The Clod*
and the Pebble', in Songs of Experience, 1794

Who can give a law to lovers? Love is a greater law unto itself.

Roman philosopher and politician **Boethius** *[c. 475–524],*
On the Consolation of Philosophy, 522

First love, with its frantic haughty imagination, swings its object clear of the everyday, over the rut of living, making him all looks, silences, gestures, attitudes, a burning phrase with no context.

Anglo-Irish novelist **Elizabeth Bowen** *[1899–1973],*
The House in Paris, 1935

> When first we met we did not guess
> That Love would prove so hard a master.

Poet **Robert Bridges** *[1844–1930], 'Triolet', 1890*

How do I love thee? Let me count the ways.
I love thee to the depth and breadth and height
My soul can reach, when feeling out of sight
For the ends of Being and ideal Grace.
I love thee with a love I seemed to lose
With my lost saints – I love thee with the breath,
Smiles, tears, of all my life! – and, if God choose,
I shall but love thee better after death.

Poet **Elizabeth Barrett Browning** *[1806–61],*
'Sonnets from the Portuguese', No. 43, 1850

Take away love and our earth is a tomb.

Poet **Robert Browning** *[1812–89]*

Ae fond kiss, and then we sever!
Ae fareweel, and then for ever!
Deep in heart-wrung tears I'll pledge thee,
Warring sighs and groans I'll wage thee . . .
Had we never lov'd sae kindly,
Had we never lov'd sae blindly,
Never met – or never parted,
We had ne'er been broken-hearted.
Scottish poet **Robert Burns** *[1759–96], 'Ae Fond Kiss', 1791*

'Tis better to have loved and lost than never to have lost at all.
Writer **Samuel Butler** *[1835–1902], The Way of All Flesh, Chapter 77, 1903*

In her first passion woman loves her lover,
In all the others all she loves is love.
Poet **George, Lord Byron** *[1788–1834], Don Juan, 1819–24*

Better be courted and jilted
Than never be courted at all.
Scottish poet **Thomas Campbell** *[1777–1844], 'The Jilted Nymph'*

Let us live, my Lesbia, and let us love, and let us reckon all the murmurs of more censorious old men as worth one farthing.
Roman poet **Catullus** *[c. 84–c. 54 BC], Carmina, No 5*

If you cannot inspire a woman with love of you, fill her above the brim with love of herself – all that runs over will be yours.

Clergyman and writer **Charles Coleb Colton**
[1780–1832], Lacon, 1829

Courtship to marriage is as a very witty prologue to a very dull play.

Playwright **William Congreve** *[1670–1729],*
The Old Bachelor, Act 5, 1693

Love all love of other sights controls,
And makes one little room an everywhere.
Poet and divine **John Donne** *[1572–1631],*
'The Good-Morrow', 1633

Pains of love be sweeter far
Than all other pleasures are.
Poet and playwright **John Dryden** *[1631–1700],*
Tyrannic Love, 1669

All mankind love a lover.
American poet and essayist **Ralph Waldo Emerson**
[1803–82], 'Love', in Essays, 1841

What is commonly called love, namely the desire of satisfying a voracious appetite with a certain quantity of delicate white human flesh.

Novelist and judge **Henry Fielding** *[1707–54],*
Tom Jones, 1749

There is hardly any activity, any enterprise, which is started with such tremendous hopes and expectations, and yet which fails so regularly, as love.

American philosopher and psychiatrist **Erich Fromm**
[1900–80], The Art of Loving, 1956

Love is the irresistible desire to be irresistibly desired.

American poet **Robert Frost** *[1874–1963]*

To love is to admire with the heart; to admire is to love with the mind.

French man of letters **Theophile Gautier** *[1811–72]*

Love has no other desire but to fulfil itself.
But if you love and must needs have desires, let these
be your desires:
To melt and be like the running brook that sings its
melody to the night.
To know the pain of too much tenderness.
To be wounded by your own understanding of love;
And to bleed willingly and joyfully.
To wake at dawn with a winged heart and give thanks
for another day of loving;
To rest at the noon hour and meditate love's ecstasy;
To return home at eventide with gratitude;
And then to sleep with a prayer for the beloved in
your heart and a song of praise upon your lips . . .

Syrian writer and artist **Kahlil Gibran** *[1883–1931],*
The Prophet, 1923

In for a penny, in for a pound –
It's love that makes the world go round.
Writer and librettist **W S Gilbert** *[1836–1911],*
Iolanthe, 1882

A man who would woo a fair maid,
Should 'prentice himself to the trade;
   And study all day,
   In methodical way,
How to flatter, cajole and persuade.
Writer and librettist **W S Gilbert** *[1836–1911],*
The Yeoman of the Guard, 1888

Love, love, love – all the wretched cant of it, masking egotism, lust, masochism, fantasy under a mythology of sentimental postures, a welter of self-induced miseries and joys, blinding and masking the essential personalities in the frozen gestures of courtship, in the kissing and the dating and the desire, the compliments and the quarrels which vivify its barrenness.
Australian feminist and academic **Germaine Greer**
[b. 1939], The Female Eunuch, 1970

Our days will be so ecstatic
Our nights will be so exotic
For I'm a neurotic erratic
And you're an erratic erotic.
America songwriter **E Y ('Yip') Harburg** *[1898–1981],*
'Courtship in Greenwich Village', 1965

And at home by the fire, whenever you look up, there I shall be – and whenever I look up there will you be.

> *Novelist and poet* **Thomas Hardy** *[1840–1928],*
> *Far from the Madding Crowd, Chapter 1, 1874,*
> *Gabriel Oak proposing to Bathsheba Everdene*

Let men tremble to win the hand of woman, unless they win along with it the utmost passion of her heart!

> *American novelist* **Nathaniel Hawthorne** *[1804–64],*
> *The Scarlet Letter, 1850*

And in that dream I dreamt – how like you this? –
Our first night years ago in that hotel
When you came with your deliberate kiss
To raise us towards the lovely and painful
Covenants of flesh; our separateness;
The respite in our dewy dreaming faces.

> *Irish poet* **Seamus Heaney** *[b. 1939], Field Work, 1979*

Love is a hole in the heart.

> *American journalist and screenwriter* **Ben Hecht**
> *[1894–1964], Winkelberg, 1950*

Love is just another dirty lie . . . I know about love. Love always hangs up behind the bathroom door. It smells like Lysol. To hell with love.

> *American novelist* **Ernest Hemingway** *[1898–1961],*
> *To Have and Have Not, 1937*

I wouldn't be too ladylike in love if I were you.
Writer and humorist **A P Herbert** *[1890–1971],*
'I Wouldn't be Too Ladylike'

'You must sit down', says Love, 'and taste my meat.'
So I did sit and eat.
Poet and clergyman **George Herbert** *[1593–1633],*
'Love: Love bade me welcome', 1633

Gather ye rosebuds while ye may,
Old Time is still a-flying;
And this same flower that smiles today,
To-morrow will be dying.
Poet and clergyman **Robert Herrick** *[1591–1674],*
'To the Virgins, to Make Much of Time', 1648

A woman might as well propose: her husband will claim
she did.
American humorist **Edgar Watson Howe** *[1853–1937],*
Country Town Sayings, 1911

Men are always doomed to be duped, not so much by
the arts of the other sex as by their own imaginations.
They are always wooing goddesses, and marrying mere
mortals.
American writer **Washington Irving** *[1783–1859],*
'Wives', in Bracebridge Hall, 1822

Love is like the measles; we all have to go through it.
Humorous writer **Jerome K Jerome** *[1859–1927],*
in Idle Thoughts of an Idle Fellow, 1886

Love's like the measles – all the worse when it comes
late in life.
Writer **Douglas Jerrold** *[1803–57], 'Love', in The Wit*
and Opinions of Douglas Jerrold, 1859

> Drink to me only with thine eyes,
> And I will pledge with mine;
> Or leave a kiss upon the cup,
> And I'll not look for wine.
> *Playwright and poet* **Ben Jonson** *[1572–1637],*
> *'To Celia', 1616*

She would go to the end of the world in a white petticoat.
Scottish magnate **Sir William Kirkcaldy** *of Grange*
[c. 1520–73], in a letter to the Earl of Bedford in 1567.
An eavesdropped remark referring to Mary Queen of Scots
and her love for Bothwell. J M Barrie, in What Every
Woman Knows, quoted it as 'I could follow you round the
world in my nightie'.

I loved Kirk so much, I would have skied down Mount
Everest in the nude with a carnation up my nose.
American beauty queen **Joyce McKinney** *[b. 1950] giving*
evidence at Epsom Magistrates Court in December 1977,
when charged with kidnapping her ex-lover, Kirk Anderson,
a Mormon missionary, and forcing him to make love to her

Come live with me, and be my love,
And we will all the pleasures prove,
That valleys, groves, hills and fields,
Woods or steepy mountains yield.
Playwright **Christopher Marlowe** *[1564–93],*
'The Passionate Shepherd to His Love', a translation of
Lucan's Pharsalia

Had we but world enough, and time,
This coyness, lady, were no crime.
Poet and politician **Andrew Marvell** *[1621–78],*
'To His Coy Mistress', 1681

Love is just a dirty trick played on us to achieve the
continuation of the species.
Novelist and short-story writer **W Somerset Maugham**
[1874–1965], A Writer's Notebook, 1949

Love is the triumph of imagination over intelligence.
American journalist and literary critic **H L Mencken**
[1880–1956]

Love is the delusion that one woman is different from
another.
American journalist and literary critic **H L Mencken**
[1880–1956], Chrestomathy, Chapter 30, 1949

There's nothing half so sweet in life
As love's young dream.
Irish poet **Thomas Moore** *[1779–1852], 'Love's Young
Dream', in Irish Melodies, 1807–35*

A man reserves his true and deepest love not for the species of woman in whose company he finds himself electrified and enkindled, but for that one in whose company he may feel tenderly drowsy.
American drama critic **George Jean Nathan**
*[1882–1958], 'The Ultimately Desirable Woman', in The
Theatre Book of the Year, 1949–1950*

Love is like quicksilver in the hand.
Leave the fingers open and it stays.
Clutch it, and it darts away.
American writer **Dorothy Parker** *[1893–1967]*

The heart has its reasons, of which reason knows nothing.
French mathematician and man of letters **Blaise Pascal**
[1623–62]

Love is not the dying moan of a distant violin – it's the triumphant twang of a bedspring.
American humorist **S J Perelman** *[1904–79]*

Love is a grave mental disease.
Greek philosopher **Plato** *[428–347 BC]*

There can be no peace of mind in love, since the advantage one has secured is never anything but a fresh starting-point for further desires.

French novelist **Marcel Proust** *[1871–1922],*
Swann in Love

Better to be an old man's darling than a young man's slave.

Proverb – *English*

He that would the daughter win,
Must with the mother first begin.

Proverb – *English*

Love makes the time pass; time makes the love pass.

Proverb – *French*

Love knows hidden paths.

Proverb – *German*

Where there is love there is pain.

Proverb – *Spanish*

But true love is a durable fire
In the mind ever burning;
Never sick, never old, never dead,
From itself never turning.

English mariner and courtier **Sir Walter Raleigh**
[c. 1552–1618], in 'Walsingham'

Love is a positive charge – if your battery isn't dead.
Motto embroidered on a cushion in the study of Scots-born
Conservative politician **Malcolm Rifkind**
[b. 1946]

Oh! she was good as she was fair.
None – none on earth above her!
As pure in thought as angels are,
To know her was to love her.
Poet **Samuel Rogers** *[1763–1855], Jacqueline, 1814*

Love is something far more than desire for sexual inter-course; it is the principal means of escape from the loneliness which afflicts more men and women through-out the greater part of their lives.
Mathematician and philosopher **Bertrand Russell**
[1872–1970], 'The Place of Love in Human Life',
in Marriage and Morals, 1929

Wou'd you in Love succeed, be Brisk, be Gay,
Cast all dull Thoughts and serious Looks away;
Think not with down cast Eyes, and mournful Air,
To move to pity, the Relentless Fair,
Or draw from her bright Eyes a Christal Tear.
Poet and courtier **Charles Sackville** *[Earl of Dorset,*
1638–1706], 'The Advice'

Life has taught us that love does not consist in gazing at each other but in looking outward together in the same direction.
French novelist and airman **Antoine de Saint-Exupery**
[1900–44], 'Wind, Sand and Stars', 1939

Love means never having to say you're sorry.
American writer **Erich Segal** *[b.1937], in the 1970 film*
Love Story, later released as a novel

Ay me! for aught that ever I could read,
Could ever hear by tale or history,
The course of true love never did run smooth.
Playwright **William Shakespeare** *[1564–1616],*
A Midsummer Night's Dream, Act 1, Scene 1, 1595–6,
Lysander speaking

If music be the food of love, play on,
Give me excess of it, that, surfeiting,
The appetite may sicken and so die.
Playwright **William Shakespeare** *[1564–1616],*
Twelfth Night, Act 1, Scene 1, 1600, Duke Orsino
speaking

Love sought is good, but giv'n unsought is better.
Playwright **William Shakespeare** *[1564–1616],*
Twelfth Night, Act 3, Scene 1, 1601,
Olivia speaking to Viola

Speak of them as they are; nothing extenuate,
Nor set down aught in malice; then must you speak
Of one that lov'd not wisely, but too well.

Playwright **William Shakespeare** *[1564–1616],*
Othello, Act V, Scene 2, Othello speaking

Give me my Romeo; and, when he shall die,
Take him and cut him out in little stars,
And he will make the face of heaven so fine
That all the world will be in love with night
And pay no worship to the garish sun.

Playwright **William Shakespeare** *[1564–1616],*
Romeo and Juliet, Act 3, Scene 2, 1595,
Juliet speaking

First love is only a little foolishness and a lot of curiosity:
no really self-respecting woman would take advantage
of it.

Irish playwright and wit **George Bernard Shaw**
[1856–1950], John Bull's Other Island, Act 4, 1907,
Broadbent speaking

Won't you come into the garden? I would like my roses
to see you.

Attributed to playwright and politician **Richard Brinsley**
Sheridan *[1751–1816], to a young lady*

I will make you brooches and toys for your delight
Of bird-song at morning and star-shine at night.
I will make a palace fit for you and me,

Of green days in forests and blue days at sea.

I will make my kitchen, and you shall keep your room,
Where white flows the river and bright blows the broom,
And you shall wash your linen and keep your body white
In rainfall at morning and dewfall at night.

And this shall be for music when no one else is near,
The fine song for singing, the rare song to hear!
That only I remember, that only you admire,
Of the broad road that stretches and the roadside fire.

Scottish writer **Robert Louis Stevenson** *[1850–94],*
'Romance'

I hold it true, whate'er befall;
I feel it, when I sorrow most;
'Tis better to have loved and lost
Than never to have loved at all.

Poet **Alfred, Lord Tennyson** *[1809–92], In Memoriam*
A.H.H., 1850, Canto 28

Some cynical Frenchman has said that there are two
parties to a love transaction: the one who loves and the
other who condescends to be so treated.

Novelist **William Makepeace Thackeray** *[1811–63],*
Vanity Fair, 1847–48

Women are well aware that what is commonly called sublime and poetical love depends not upon moral qualities, but on frequent meetings, and on the style in which the hair is done up, and on the colour and the cut of the dress.

Russian novelist **Leo Tolstoy** *[1828–1910],*
The Kreutzer Sonata, 1890

Love is being stupid together.

French poet and essayist **Paul Valéry** *[1871–1945]*

'Love' is the same as 'like', except you feel sexier.

American poet **Judith Viorst** *[b. 1931]*

Infatuation is when you think he's as sexy as Robert Redford, as smart as Henry Kissinger, as noble as Ralph Nader, as funny as Woody Allen and as athletic as Jimmy Connors. Love is when you realize that he's as sexy as Woody Allen, as smart as Jimmy Connors, as athletic as Henry Kissinger and nothing like Robert Redford – but you'll take him anyway.

American poet **Judith Viorst** *[b. 1931]*

Love conquers all: let us too give in to love. – *Omnia vincit Amor: et nos cedamus Amori.*

Roman poet **Virgil** *[70–19 BC], Eclogues, No. 10*

Love conquers all things except poverty and toothache.

Vaudeville and film actress **Mae West** *[1893–1980]*

When one is in love one begins by deceiving oneself. And one ends by deceiving others. That is what the world calls a romance.

Irish playwright and wit **Oscar Wilde** *[1854–1900],*
A Woman of No Importance, 1893

The love that dare not speak its name.

Oscar Wilde *[1854–1900], defending himself in the dock against charges of sodomy. The phrase had been used by Lord Alfred Douglas [1870–1945] in a poem entitled 'Two Loves', 1892–3, and Wilde was challenged to explain the final line in it – 'I am the love that dare not speak its name'.*

There is a land of the living and a land of the dead, and the bridge is love, the only survival, the only meaning.

American playwright **Thornton Wilder** *[1897–1975],*
The Bridge of San Luis Rey, 1927, closing sentence

'Love,' she said, 'seems to pump me full of vitamins. It makes me feel as if the sun were shining and my hat was right and my shoes were right and my frock was right and my stockings were right, and somebody had just left me ten thousand a year.'

Novelist **P G Wodehouse** *[1881–1975]*

A pity beyond all telling
Is in the heart of love.

Irish poet **William Butler Yeats** *[1865–1939],*
'The Pity of Love', 1893

You can't buy love, but you can pay heavily for it.
American comedian **Henny Youngman** *[1906–98]*

14

Marriage

Marriage is the tomb of love. (Proverb – Russian)

Sorry to start on such a gloomy note about marriage – but it is astonishing how many writers and thinkers, both men and women, regard (or affect to regard) the institution of matrimony as a mausoleum of all the hopes and joys of love. 'Wedded bliss' and 'happy ever after' seem to belong only to folklore and fairytale. Only the Bible has a really good word for it. Yet the word 'matrimony', the state of being married, is honourably sprung from the Latin word for 'mother' (*mater*), whereas 'patrimony' (derived from 'father') expresses the much more mundane concept of property inherited from ancestors. But is wedlock *really* synonymous with deadlock? Is marriage *really* a state of quiet but irredeemable despair? Who speaks for the millions who have not only survived but enjoyed decades of marriage? They're out there, somewhere.

" "

I think the secret of a long marriage is knowing how to say 'Yes, dear'.
American actor **Ben Affleck** *[b. 1972], Hello! magazine,*
May 1999

An optimist is a man who believes that he can marry his secretary and keep on dictating to her.
Anon

Bigamy is having one husband too many; monogamy is the same.
Anon, *quoted as the epigraph to Fear of Flying by American writer Erica Jong [b. 1942]*

Marriage is too important to be treated like a love affair.
Anon, *quoted by journalist Katharine Whitehorn [b. 1928] in the Observer, 1 March 1992*

Love is blind but marriage restores the sight.
Anon

Never argue with your wife – it's just your word against hundreds of hers.
Anon

To marry a man out of pity is folly; and, if you think you are going to influence the kind of fellow who has 'never had a chance, poor devil', you are profoundly mistaken. One can only influence the strong characters in life, not the weak; and it is the height of vanity to suppose that you can make an honest man of anyone.

Scottish political hostess and writer **Margot Asquith** *[1864–1945], The Autobiography of Margot Asquith, 1920*

I married beneath me. All women do.

Conservative politician **Lady Nancy Astor** *[1879–1964], in a speech in Oldham in 1951*

In all the important preparations of the mind she was complete; being prepared for matrimony by a hatred of home, restraint and tranquillity; by the misery of disappointed affection, and contempt of the man she was to marry.

Novelist **Jane Austen** *[1775–1817], Mansfield Park, said of Maria Bertram*

Happiness in marriage is entirely a matter of chance.

Novelist **Jane Austen** *[1775–1817], Pride and Prejudice, 1813*

Wives are young men's mistresses, companions for middle age, and old men's nurses.

Philosopher, courtier and politician **Francis Bacon** *[1561–1626], 'Of Marriage and Single Life' in Essays, 1625*

A princely marriage is the brilliant edition of a universal fact, and as such, it rivets mankind.

> *Constitutional historian* **Walter Bagehot** *[1826–77],*
> *in The English Constitution, 1867*

The majority of husbands remind me of an orang-utan trying to play the violin.

> *French writer* **Honoré de Balzac** *[1799–1850],*
> *The Physiology of Marriage, 1826*

The fate of a marriage depends on the first night.

> *French writer* **Honoré de Balzac** *[1799–1850],*
> *The Physiology of Marriage, 1826*

I am now more than fifty years of age, and if you ask me what are the immutable rules of marriage, I can think of only one: a man never leaves his wife for an older woman. Apart from that, anything that is possible is normal.

> *Novelist* **Julian Barnes** *[b. 1946], Talking It Over,*
> *Chapter 12, 1991, Mme Marie-Christine Wyatt, having*
> *been left by her husband for a younger woman*

Marriage always demands the greatest understanding of the art of insincerity possible between two human beings.

> *American writer* **Vicki Baum** *[1888–1960],*
> *And Life Goes On, 1931*

I've known for years our marriage has been a mockery.
My body lying there night after night in the wasted
moonlight. I know now how the Taj Mahal must
feel.

Playwright and actor **Alan Bennett** *[b. 1934],*
Habeas Corpus, 1973

Therefore shall a man leave his father and his mother,
and shall cleave unto his wife: and they shall be one flesh.

Bible, *Genesis 2:24*

It is better to marry than to burn.

Bible, *1 Corinthians 7:9*

Marriage, *n*: the state or condition of a community
consisting of a master, a mistress and two slaves, making
in all, two.

American journalist **Ambrose Bierce** *[1842–1914],*
The Devil's Dictionary, 1911

No modern woman with a grain of sense ever sends little
notes to an unmarried man – not until she is married,
anyway.

Journalist **Arthur Binstead** *['The Pitcher',*
1861–1914], Pitcher's Proverbs, 1909

That is partly why women marry – to keep up the fiction
of being in the hub of things.

Anglo-Irish novelist **Elizabeth Bowen** *[1899–1973],*
The House in Paris, 1935

One was never married, and that's his hell; another is, and that's his plague.

> *Clergyman and writer* **Robert Burton** *[1577–1640]*,
> *The Anatomy of Melancholy, 1621*

Romances paint at full length people's wooings,
But only give a bust of marriages:
For no one cares for matrimonial cooings.
There's nothing wrong in a connubial kiss:
Think you, if Laura had been Petrarch's wife,
He would have written sonnets all his life?

> *Poet* **George, Lord Byron** *[1788–1824], Don Juan*,
> *1824*

I shall marry in haste, and repeat at leisure.

> *American fantasy novelist* **James Branch Cabell**
> *[1879–1958]*

(Marriage is) the deep, deep peace of the double-bed after the hurly-burly of the chaise-longue.

> *Actress* **Mrs Patrick Campbell** *[Beatrice Stella Campbell, 1865–1940], cited in Alexander Woollcott, 'The First Mrs Tanqueray', in While Rome Burns, 1934*

It's too bad that in most marriage ceremonies they don't use the word 'obey' any more. It used to lend a little humour to the occasion.

> *American marriage counsellor* **Lloyd Cary**

There is one good wife in the country, and every man thinks he hath her.

Spanish novelist **Miguel de Cervantes** *[1547–1616],*
Don Quixote, 1620

We wedded men live in sorrow and care.

Poet **Geoffrey Chaucer** *[1340–1410]*

If you are afraid of loneliness, don't get married.

Russian playwright **Anton Chekhov** *[1860–1904],*
Nauka

Marriage is an adventure, like going to war.

Poet and novelist **G K Chesterton** *[1874–1936]*

Dear God. The people in the next apartment fight real loud all the time. You should only let very good friends get married. Nan.

From **Children's Letters to God***, Eric Marshall and*
Stewart Hample, 1975

Dear God. I went to this wedding and they kissed right in church. Is that O.K. Neil.

From **Children's Letters to God***, Eric Marshall and*
Stewart Hample, 1975

An archaeologist is the best husband any woman can have: the older she gets, the more interested he is in her.

Attributed to detective novelist **Agatha Christie**
[1890–1976], who was married to archaeologist
Max Mallowan. Quoted in a news report in March 1954,
but vehemently refuted by her

The state of having only one spouse is called monotony.
Classroom howler

The most happy marriage I can picture or imagine to myself would be the union of a deaf man to a blind woman.

Attributed to poet **Samuel Taylor Coleridge**
[1772–1834]

The dread of loneliness is greater than the fear of bondage, so we get married.

Writer and critic **Cyril Connolly** *[1903–75],*
The Unquiet Grave, 1945

We sleep in separate rooms, we have dinner apart, we take separate vacations. We're doing everything we can to keep our marriage together.

American comedian **Rodney Dangerfield** *[b. 1921]*

I'd marry again if I found a man who had fifteen million dollars, would sign over half of it to me before the marriage, and guarantee he'd be dead within a year.

American film actress **Bette Davis** *[1908–89]*

The tragedy of marriage is that while women marry thinking that their man will change, all men marry believing that their wife will never change. Both are invariably disappointed.

> *Espionage fiction writer* **Len Deighton** *[b. 1929],*
> *London Match, 1986*

I have always thought that every woman should marry, and no man.

> *Prime Minister and novelist* **Benjamin Disraeli**
> *[1804–81], Lothair, 1870*

When you're married to someone, they take you for granted . . . when you're living with someone it's fantastic . . . they're so frightened of losing you they've got to keep you satisfied all the time.

> *Novelist and playwright* **Nell Dunn** *[b. 1936], Poor Cow,*
> *1967*

His designs were strictly honourable, as the phrase is: that is, to rob a lady of her fortune by way of marriage.

> *Novelist and judge* **Henry Fielding** *[1707–54],*
> *Tom Jones, 1749*

Keep your eyes wide open before marriage, half-shut afterwards.

> *American inventor and politician* **Benjamin Franklin**
> *[1706–90], Poor Richard's Almanack, June 1738*

A man in love is incomplete until he is married. Then he is finished.

> *Hungarian film-star* **Zsa Zsa Gabor** *[b. c. 1919]*,
> *Newsweek, 1960*

You shall be together when the white wings of death
  scatter your days.
Ay, you shall be together even in the silent memory
  of God,
But let there be spaces in your togetherness,
And let the winds of the heavens dance between you.

> *Syrian writer and artist* **Kahlil Gibran** *[1883–1931]*,
> *'On Marriage', in The Prophet, 1923*

The trouble with marrying your mistress is that you create a job vacancy.

> *Attributed to business tycoon* **James Goldsmith**
> *[1933–97]*

When a man steals your wife, there is no better revenge than to let him keep her.

> *French actor and playwright* **Sacha Guitry**
> *[1885–1957], Elles et toi, 1948*

My mother said it was simple to keep a man: you must be a maid in the living room, a cook in the kitchen and a whore in the bedroom. I said I'd hire the other two and take care of the bedroom bit myself.

> *American model* **Jerry Hall** *[b. 1957]*

I do not refer to myself as a 'housewife' for the reason that I did not marry a house.

American feminist **Wilma Scott Heide** *[1926–85]*

If men knew how women pass the time when they are alone, they'd never marry.

American writer **O Henry** *[1862–1910], 'Memoirs of a Yellow Dog', Four Million, 1906*

The critical period in matrimony is breakfast-time.

Writer and humorist **A P Herbert** *[1890–1971], 'Is Marriage Lawful?', Uncommon Law, 1935*

Marriage: the conventional ending of a love affair. A lonesome state.

American anthologists **Oliver Herford** *[1863–1935] and* **John C Clay**, *Cupid's Cyclopaedia, 1910*

Mom and Pop were just a couple of kids when they got married. He was eighteen, she was sixteen, and I was three.

American Blues singer **Billie Holiday** *[1915–59], the opening words of her autobiography Lady Sings the Blues, 1958*

Marriage is a good deal like a circus: there is not as much in it as is represented in the advertising.

American humorist **Edgar Watson Howe** *[1853–1937], Country Town Sayings, 1911*

A gentleman who had been very unhappy in marriage, married immediately after his wife died. Johnson said it was the triumph of hope over experience.

Author and lexicographer **Samuel Johnson** *[1709–84],*
quoted by James Boswell, The Life of Samuel Johnson
(1791), in 1770

The most difficult year of marriage is the one you're in.

American actor **Franklin Pierce Jones** *[1853–1935]*

Seldom, or perhaps never, does a marriage develop into an individual relationship smoothly and without crises; there is no coming to consciousness without pain.

Swiss psychiatrist **Carl Jung** *[1875–1961]*

Any woman who still thinks marriage is a fifty-fifty proposition is only proving that she doesn't understand either men or percentages.

American lawyer, feminist and civil rights activist
Florynce R Kennedy *[1916–2000]*

You may carve it on his tombstone, you may cut it on his
card
That a young man married is a young man marred.

Poet and novelist **Rudyard Kipling** *[1865–1936],*
'The Story of the Gadsbys', 1889

(Marriage is) one year of flames and thirty of ashes.

Attributed to Italian novelist **Giuseppe Di Lampedusa**
[1896–1957], author of The Leopard, 1957

The poor wish to be rich, the rich wish to be happy, the single wish to be married, and the married wish to be dead.
Advice columnist **Ann Landers** *[Esther Pauline Friedman Lederer, 1918–2002]*

Many a man in love with a dimple makes the mistake of marrying the whole girl.
Canadian humorist **Stephen Leacock** *[1869–1944], in Literary Lapses, 1910*

Marriage is a triumph of habit over hate.
American pianist and composer **Oscar Levant** *[1906–72], in Memoirs of an Amnesiac, 1965*

Marriage is neither heaven nor hell. It is simply purgatory.
Attributed to US President **Abraham Lincoln** *[1809–65]*

I've been married six months. She looks like a million dollars, but she only knows a hundred and twenty words and she's only got two ideas in her head. The other one is hats.
Scottish novelist **Eric Linklater** *[1899–1974], Juan in America, Chapter 5, 1931, Isidore Cohen speaking*

My wife and I had words – but I never got to use mine.
American comedy character **Fibber McGee**, *in the*
American radio show Fibber McGee and Molly
[1935–56], by Jim and Marian Jordan

Marriage was all a woman's idea, and for men's acceptance of the pretty yoke it becomes us to be grateful.
American poet **Phyllis McGinley** *[1905–78], 'How to Get Along with Men', in The Province of the Heart, 1959*

There are four stages to a marriage. First there's the affair, then there's the marriage, then children and finally the fourth stage, without which you cannot know a woman, the divorce.
American author **Norman Mailer** *[b. 1923], in Nova magazine, 1969*

A man marries to have a home, but also because he doesn't want to be bothered with sex and all that sort of thing.
Novelist and short-story writer **W Somerset Maugham** *[1874–1965], The Circle, 1921*

Marriage, if one will face the truth, is an evil, but a necessary evil.
Greek comic dramatist **Menander** *[342–c. 292 BC]*

The longest sentence you can form with two words is 'I do'.
American journalist and literary critic
H L Mencken *[1880–1956]*

The moral regeneration of mankind will only really commence, when the most fundamental of the social relations (marriage) is placed under the rule of equal justice, and when human beings learn to cultivate their strongest sympathy with an equal in rights and cultivation.

> *Philosopher and social reformer* **John Stuart Mill**
> *[1806–73], The Subjection of Women, 1869*

I am much too interested in other men's wives to think of getting one of my own.

> *Irish author* **George Moore** *[1852–1933]*

Marriage is based on the theory that when a man discovers a particular brand of beer exactly to his taste he should at once throw up his job and go to work in the brewery.

> *American drama critic* **George Jean Nathan**
> *[1882–1958], 'General Conclusions about the Coarse Sex',*
> *in The Theatre, the Drama, the Girls, 1921*

> To keep your marriage brimming
> With love in the wedding cup,
> Whenever you're wrong, admit it,
> Whenever you're right – shut up.
> *American humorist* **Ogden Nash** *[1902–71]*

He tells you when you've got on too much lipstick,
And helps you with your girdle when your hips stick.

> *American humorist* **Ogden Nash** *[1902–71],*
> *'The Perfect Husband', 1949*

If you would marry suitably, marry your equal.
Roman poet **Ovid** *[43 BC – AD c. 17]*

Strange to say what delight we married people have to see these poor fools decoyed into our condition.
Diarist and civil servant **Samuel Pepys** *[1633–1703],*
Diary: 25 December 1665, after attending a wedding

Love is the star men look up to as they walk along, and marriage is the hole they fall into.
Proverb – *Arabic*

Marry in haste and repent at leisure.
Proverb – *English*

Marriage is such a heavy burden, it takes three people to carry it.
Proverb – *French*

When an old man marries, death laughs.
Proverb – *German*

Wives and watermelons are picked by chance.
Proverb – *Greek*

Advice to persons about to marry – Don't.
Punch, *Vol 8, 1845*

It doesn't much signify whom one marries, for one is sure to find next morning that it was someone else.
Poet **Samuel Rogers** *[1763–1855], in The Table-Talk of Samuel Rogers, 1856*

I am the only man in the world with a marriage license made out 'to whom it may concern'.
American film actor **Mickey Rooney** *[b. 1920]*

A husband is what is left of a lover once the nerve has been extracted.
Anglo-American writer **Helen Rowland** *[1875–1950], in A Guide to Men, 1922*

Never trust a husband too far or a bachelor too near.
Anglo-American writer **Helen Rowland** *[1875–1950]*

Marriage is for women the commonest mode of livelihood, and the total amount of undesired sex endured by women is probably greater in marriage than in prostitution.
Mathematician and philosopher **Bertrand Russell** *[1872–1970], 'Prostitution', in Marriage and Morals, 1929*

Thy husband is thy lord, thy life, thy keeper,
Thy head, thy sovereign; one that cares for thee,
And for thy maintenance; commits his body
To painful labour both by sea and land,
To watch the night in storms, the day in cold,

Whilst thou liest warm at home, secure and safe;
And craves no other tribute at thy hands
But love, fair looks, and true obedience, –
Too little payment for so great a debt!
Playwright **William Shakespeare** *[1564–1616],*
The Taming of the Shrew, Act V, Scene 2, Katharina
speaking

Marriage is popular because it combines the maximum
of temptation with the maximum of opportunity.
Irish playwright and critic **George Bernard Shaw**
[1856–1950], 'Maxims for Revolutionists', in Man and
Superman, 1903

The one point on which all women are in furious secret
rebellion against the existing law is the saddling of the
right to a child with the obligation to become the servant
of a man.
Irish playwright and critic **George Bernard Shaw**
[1856–1950], Preface, 'The Right to Motherhood',
Getting Married, 1931

A system could not well have been devised more
studiously hostile to human happiness than marriage.
Poet **Percy Bysshe Shelley** *[1792–1822]*

Married women are kept women, and they are beginning
to find it out.
American writer **Logan Pearsall Smith** *[1865–1946],*
Afterthoughts

(Marriage) resembles a pair of shears, so joined that they cannot be separated; often moving in opposite directions, yet always punishing anyone who comes between them.

Clergyman, writer and wit **Sydney Smith** *[1771–1845], in Holland, A Memoir of the Reverend Sydney Smith, 1855*

By all means marry. If you get a good wife, you'll become happy; if you get a bad one, you'll become a philosopher.

Greek philosopher **Socrates** *[469–399 BC]*

I can't mate in captivity.

American feminist writer and activist **Gloria Steinem** *[b. 1934]*

Some of us are becoming the men we wanted to marry.

American feminist writer and activist **Gloria Steinem** *[b. 1934]*

Marriage is one long conversation, chequered by disputes. Two persons more and more adapt their notions to suit the other, and in the process of time, without sound of trumpets, they conduct each other into new worlds of thought.

Scottish writer **Robert Louis Stevenson** *[1650–94]*

(Marriage) hath in it less of beauty but more of safety than the single life; it hath more care, but less danger; it is more merry, and more sad; it is fuller of sorrows, and fuller of joys; it lies under more burdens, but is supported by all the strengths of love and charity, and these burdens are delightful.

Clergyman and bishop **Jeremy Taylor** *[1613–67]*

It is better to marry only because it is worse to burn. It is still better neither to marry nor to burn.

Latin Church father **Tertullian** *[160–c. 225]*

Take it from me – marriage isn't a word, it's a sentence.

American film-maker **King Vidor** *[1894–1982], in The Crawl, 1928 film*

A fool and his money are soon married.

American writer **Carolyn Wells** *[1870–1942]*

Marriage is a great institution, but I'm not ready for an institution yet.

Attributed to American vaudeville and film actress **Mae West** *[1893–1980]*

There is nothing in the world like the devotion of a married woman. It's a thing no married man knows anything about.

Irish playwright and wit **Oscar Wilde** *[1854–1900], Lady Windermere's Fan, 1893*

The one charm of marriage is that it makes a life of deception absolutely necessary for both parties.
Irish playwright and wit **Oscar Wilde** *[1854–1900],*
The Picture of Dorian Gray, 1891

Marriage is a bribe to make a housekeeper think she is a householder.
American novelist and playwright **Thornton Wilder**
[1897–1975], The Merchant of Yonkers, 1939

I married him for better or worse, but not for lunch.
Attributed to the **Duchess of Windsor** *[1896–1986],*
about her husband the Duke – she liked lunching out, he
liked lunching in

All marriages are happy. It's trying to live together afterwards that causes all the problems.
American film actress **Shelley Winters** *[b. 1922]*

15

Divorce

He taught me housekeeping; when I divorce, I keep the house. (Hungarian-born actress **Zsa Zsa Gabor** (b. c. 1919), about her fifth husband)

The watershed year was 1969 – the year of the Divorce Reform Act, which introduced the key concept of the right to a divorce if both partners wish it, without legal guilt on either side. Before that, divorce had been available only through an expensive resort to Parliament (1603–1857), or through a common law action of 'criminal conversation', brought by a husband against another man for adultery with his wife (a trespass on his property). The year 1857 brought the Matrimonial Causes Act, which allowed husbands (but not wives) to obtain a divorce on the grounds of a single act of adultery by the wife (the wife was allowed the same privilege in 1923). It led to the absurd charade of people fabricating 'evidence' of adultery in seedy hotels. Even though divorce is a much more 'civilised' proceeding now (one in three marriages in Britain end in divorce, some after only a year of marriage), it is still a deeply unhappy topic. It is impossible to contemplate the word itself without thinking with dismay of the pain and heartache which can attend the ending of a marriage – any marriage – for the couple involved and for their children.

66 99

I read about divorce, and I can't see why two people can't get along together in harmony, and I see two people and I can't see how either of them can live with the other.
American journalist and humorous writer **Franklin P Adams** *[1881–1960], Nods and Becks, 1944*

A divorce is like an amputation; you survive, but there's less of you.
Canadian writer and critic **Margaret Atwood** *[b. 1939] in Time, March 1987*

My wife and I have been married for forty-seven years and not once have we had an argument serious enough to consider divorce; murder, yes, but divorce, never.
American comedian **Jack Benny** *[1894–1974]*

What therefore God hath joined together, let not man put asunder.
Bible, *Matthew 19:6*

The difference between divorce and legal separation is that a legal separation gives a husband time to hide his money.

American television presenter **Johnny Carson** *[b. 1925]*

The only solid and lasting peace between a man and his wife is, doubtless, a separation.

Politician and writer **Lord Chesterfield** *[1694–1773],*
Letters to His Son, 1 September 1763

Divorce is a system whereby two people make a mistake and one of them goes on paying for it.

Espionage fiction writer **Len Deighton** *[b. 1929], cited*
in A Alvarez, Life after Marriage

Our marriage is dead, when pleasure is fled:
'Twas pleasure first made it an oath.

Poet and playwright **John Dryden** *[1631–1700],*
Songs, 1673

Better a tooth out than always aching.

Writer and physician **Thomas Fuller** *[1654–1734],*
Gnomologia, 1732

I never hated a man enough to give him diamonds back.'

Hungarian-born actress **Zsa Zsa Gabor** *[b. c. 1919],*
in the Observer, 25 August 1957

The happiest time of anyone's life is just after the first divorce.

Canadian-born American economist **John Kenneth Galbraith** *[b. 1908]*

My notion of a wife at forty is that a man should be able to change her, like a bank note, for two twenties.

Writer **Douglas Jerrold** *[1803–37]*

Nature has given women so much power that the law has very wisely given them little.

Writer and lexicographer **Samuel Johnson** *[1709–84]*

An open marriage is Nature's way of telling you that you need a divorce.

Advice columnist **Ann Landers** *[Esther Pauline Friedman Lederer, 1918–2002]*

There is one thing I would break up over, and that is if she caught me with another woman. I wouldn't stand for that.

American actor **Steve Martin** *[b. 1945]*

Alimony: the ransom the happy pay to the devil.

American journalist and literary critic **H L Mencken** *[1880–1956], 'Sententiae', in A Book of Burlesques, 1920*

When a couple decide to divorce, they should inform both sets of parents before having a party and telling all their friends. This is not only courteous but practical.

198

Parents may be very willing to pitch in with comments, criticism and malicious gossip of their own to help the divorce along.

American humorist **P J O'Rourke** *[b. 1947]*

All this divorce – when I meet a man now the first thing I think about is 'Is this the sort of man I want my children to spend their weekends with?'

American comedienne and essayist **Rita Rudner** *[b. 1956]*

Felix: Oh, I'm awfully sorry. It's a terrible thing, isn't it? Divorce?

Gwendolin: It can be . . . if you haven't got the right solicitor.

Playwright **Neil Simon** *[b. 1927], The Odd Couple, 1966*

Divorce is probably of nearly the same date as marriage. I believe, however, that marriage is by some weeks the more ancient.

French writer and philosopher **Voltaire** *[1694–1778],*
Philosophical Dictionary, 1764

If our divorce laws were improved, we could at least say that if marriage does nobody much good it does nobody any harm.

Author **Rebecca West** *[1892–1983], The Clarion*

Divorces are made in heaven.

Attributed to Irish playwright and wit **Oscar Wilde**
[1854–1900]

16

Parents and grandparents

Father doesn't hear what Mother says, and Mother hears what Father doesn't say. (Anon)

Grandparents are on the up and up. Apparently, one in three people in the UK is a grandparent. So there are a lot of us around. Ask any grandmother or grandfather, and it's odds-on that they will say that they find grandparenthood even more fulfilling than parenthood. It's not surprising, perhaps; there is less constant pressure, less daily hassle, lighter responsibilities, more time to enjoy the company of the youngsters within (mercifully?) finite limits. And yet, and yet – it is not merely sentimentality to recall, amid the trials and tribulations of child-rearing, the intense delights and the soaring pride in achievement (the children's, not yours), the shared hopes and fears, the profound and enduring satisfactions of parenthood. For every cynic or sceptic who puts pen to paper on the subject of parenthood, there are countless others who quietly cherish the joy which parenthood has brought them.

66 99

The joys of parents are secret, and so are their griefs and fears; they cannot utter the one, nor will they not utter the other.
Philosopher and politician **Francis Bacon** *[1561–1626],*
'Of Parents and Children', Essays, 1625

We never know the love of our parents for us until we have become parents.
American Congregationalist clergyman and writer **Henry Ward Beecher** *[1813–87], Proverbs from Plymouth Pulpit, 1887*

Children always assume that the sexual lives of their parents come to a grinding halt at their conception.
Playwright and actor **Alan Bennett** *[b. 1934], Getting On, 1972*

Honour thy father and thy mother: that thy days may be long upon the land which the Lord thy God giveth thee.
Bible, *Exodus 20:12*

Despise not thy mother when she is old.
Bible, *Proverbs 23:22*

Some are kissing mothers and some are scolding mothers, but it is love just the same, and most mothers kiss and scold together.

American novelist **Pearl S Buck** *[1892–1973], 'To You on Your First Birthday', To My Daughters, With Love, 1967*

Parents are the last people on earth who ought to have children.

Attributed to author **Samuel Butler** *[1835–1902]*

Human beings are the only creatures which allow their children to come back home.

American actor and comedian **Bill Cosby** *[b. 1937], in Fatherhood, 1986*

The first half of our lives is ruined by our parents, and the second half by our children.

American lawyer, agnostic and reformer **Clarence Darrow** *[1857–1938]*

There are times when parenthood seems nothing more than feeding the mouth that bites you.

American novelist and humorist **Peter De Vries** *[1910–93], Tunnel of Love, Chapter 5*

Nobody can misunderstand a boy like his own mother.

Scottish novelist and essayist **Norman Douglas** *[1868–1952]*

Having one child makes you a parent; having two, you are a referee.

> Broadcaster **David Frost** *[b. 1939], quoted in the Independent, 16 September 1989*

Where yet was ever found a mother,
Who'd give her booby (baby) for another?

Poet and dramatist **John Gay** *[1685–1732], 'The Mother, the Nurse, and the Fairy', in Fables, 1727–38*

Leontine: An only son, sir, might expect more indulgence.
Croaker: An only father, sir, might expect more obedience.

> *Irish-born writer and playwright* **Oliver Goldsmith** *[1730–74], in The Good-natur'd Man, 1768*

Mother is the dead heart of the family, spending father's earnings on consumer goods to enhance the environment in which he eats, sleeps and watches television.

> *Australian feminist writer and academic* **Germaine Greer** *[b. 1939], The Female Eunuch, 1970*

One father is more than a hundred schoolmasters.

> *Poet and clergyman* **George Herbert** *[1593–1633], Jacula Prudentum, No. 686, 1651*

A mother never realises that her children are no longer children.

> *Journalist and editor* **Holbrook Jackson** *[1874–1948], 'On a Certain Arrangement', in All Manner of Folk, 1912*

One parent is enough to spoil you but discipline takes two.

Australian-born broadcaster **Clive James** *[b. 1939],*
Unreliable Memoirs

The real menace in dealing with a five-year-old is that in no time at all you begin to sound like a five-year-old.

American writer and lyricist **Jean Kerr** *[1922–2003],*
'How to Get the Best out of Your Children', in Please Don't
Eat the Daisies, 1957

> They fuck you up, your mum and dad.
> They may not mean to, but they do.
> They fill you with the faults they had
> And add some extra, just for you.

Poet **Philip Larkin** *[1922–85], 'This Be the Verse', 1974*

A wise man once said that next to losing its mother, there is nothing more healthy for a child than to lose its father. And though I would never subscribe to such a statement wholeheartedly, I would be the last person to reject it out of hand. For my own part, I would express such a doctrine without any suggestion of bitterness against the world, or rather without the hurt which the mere sound of the words implies.

Icelandic novelist **Halldór Laxness** *[1902–98],*
The Fish Can Sing, 1957, opening lines

The simplest toy, one which even the youngest child can operate, is called a grandparent.

American humorist **Sam Levenson** *[1911–80],*
You Don't Have to Be in Who's Who to Know
What's What

In the dark womb where I began
My mother's life made me a man.
Through all the months of human birth
Her beauty fed my common earth.
I cannot see, nor breathe, nor stir,
But through the death of some of her.

Poet and novelist **John Masefield** *[1878–1967],*
'C.L.M', in Ballads and Poems, 1910

D'you call life a bad job? Never! We've had our ups and downs, we've had our struggles, we've always been poor, but it's been worth it, ay, worth it a hundred times I say when I look round at my children.

Novelist and short-story writer **W Somerset Maugham**
[1874–1965], Of Human Bondage, 1915

Few misfortunes can befall a boy which bring worse consequences than to have a really affectionate mother.

Novelist and short-story writer **W Somerset Maugham**
[1874–1965], A Writer's Notebook, 1896,
published in 1949

He is too experienced a parent ever to make positive promises.

> *American writer* **Christopher Morley** *[1890–1957],*
> *Thunder on the Left*

Every generation revolts against its fathers and makes friends with its grandfathers.

> *American sociologist* **Lewis Mumford** *[1895–1990],*
> *The Brown Decades, 1931*

Children aren't happy without something to ignore,
And that's what parents were created for.

> *American poet* **Ogden Nash** *[1902–71], 'The Parent',*
> *in Happy Days, 1933*

Oh, what a tangled web do parents weave
When they think that their children are naïve.

> *American poet* **Ogden Nash** *[1902–71], 'Baby, What*
> *Makes the Sky Blue', 1940*

Because of their size parents may be difficult to discipline properly.

> *American humorist* **P J O'Rourke** *[b. 1947], Modern*
> *Manners, 1984*

Prentice: You did have a father?
Geraldine: Oh, I'm sure I did. My mother was frugal in her habits, but she'd never economise unwisely.

> *Playwright* **Joe Orton** *[1933–67], in What the Butler*
> *Saw*

All the same, you know, parents – especially step-parents – are sometimes a bit of a disappointment to their children. They don't fulfil the promise of their early years.
Novelist **Anthony Powell** *[1905–2000], A Buyer's Market, Chapter 2, 1952*

For all of us, kisses seemed to spring from her eyes, which could not look upon those she loved without seeming to bestow upon them passionate caresses.
French novelist **Marcel Proust** *[1871–1922], 'Swann's Way', in 'Remembrance of Things Past', Swann talking about his grandmother, Bathilde*

A rich child often sits in a poor mother's lap.
Proverb *– Danish*

A father is a banker provided by nature.
Proverb *– French*

Perfect love sometimes does not come till the first grandchild.
Proverb *– Welsh*

> Your Lord has decreed
> That you worship none other but Him,
> And that you be kind
> To parents. Whether one
> Or both of them attain
> Old age in your life.
> Say not to them a word

Of contempt, nor repel them,
But address them
In terms of honour.

Qur'an, 17:23

A mother has an innate ability for aggravating the wounds of her offspring's pride. This is inevitable since the relationship between mother and child is a most unnatural one; other species have the good sense to banish their young at an early age.

Writer **John Rae** *[b. 1931], The Custard Boys,*
Chapter 13, 1960

Elephants and grandchildren never forget.

American humorist **Andy Rooney** *[b. 1919]*

A Jewish man with parents alive is a fifteen-year-old boy, and will remain a fifteen-year-old boy until *they die*!

American novelist **Philip Roth** *[b. 1933],*
Portnoy's Complaint, 1967

The fundamental defect of fathers, in our competitive society, is that they want their children to be a credit to them.

Philosopher and mathematician **Bertrand Russell**
[1872–1970], 'Freedom versus Authority in Education',
Sceptical Essays, 1928

Children are given to us to discourage our better emotions.

Scottish writer **Saki** *[H H Munro, 1870–1916],*
Reginald, 1904

No matter how old a mother is, she watches her middle-aged children for signs of improvement.

Writer **Florida Scott-Maxwell** *[1884–1979],*
The Measure of My Days, 1968

It is a wise father that knows his own child.

Playwright **William Shakespeare** *[1564–1616],*
The Merchant of Venice, Act 2, Scene 2, Launcelot Gobbo
to his father Gobbo

Thou art thy mother's glass, and she in thee
Calls back the lovely April of her prime.

Playwright **William Shakespeare** *[1564–1616],*
Sonnet 3

Parentage is a very important profession, but no test of fitness for it is ever imposed in the interest of the children.

Irish playwright and critic **George Bernard Shaw** *[1856–*
1950], in Everybody's Political What's What?, 1944

Parents learn a lot from their children about coping with life.

Scottish novelist **Muriel Spark** *[b. 1918],*
in The Comforters, Chapter 6, 1957

The more people have studied different methods of bringing up children, the more they have come to the conclusion that what good mothers and fathers instinctively feel like doing for their babies is the best after all.

American paediatrician and writer **Benjamin Spock**
[1903–98]

I wish either my father or my mother, or indeed both of them, as they were in duty both equally bound to it, had minded what they were about when they begot me.

Irish novelist **Laurence Sterne** *[1713–68],*
Tristram Shandy, 1759–67

Who ran to help me when I fell,
And would some pretty story tell,
Or kiss the place to make it well?
My Mother.

Children's books writers **Ann Taylor** *[1782–1866]*
and **Jane Taylor** *[1783–1824], 'My Mother', in Original*
Poems for Infant Minds, 1804

When I was a boy of fourteen, my father was so ignorant I could hardly stand to have the old man around. But when I got to be twenty-one, I was astonished at how much the old man had learned in seven years.

Attributed to American writer **Mark Twain**
[Samuel Langhorne Clemens, 1835–1910], whose father
died when Twain was eleven years old!

The young need old men. They need men who are not ashamed of age, not pathetic imitations of themselves . . . Parents are the bones on which children sharpen their teeth.

Actor and writer **Peter Ustinov** *[1921–2004], Dear Me, Chapter 18, 1977*

Never have children, only grandchildren.

American writer **Gore Vidal** *[b. 1925], Two Sisters, 1970*

> We have a beautiful
> mother
> Her green lap
> immense
> Her brown embrace
> eternal
> Her blue body
> everything
> we know.

American poet **Alice Walker** *[b. 1944], 'We Have a Beautiful Mother', 1991*

> A mighty power and stronger
> Man from his throne has hurled,
> For the hand that rocks the cradle
> Is the hand that rules the world.

American poet **William Ross Wallace** *[1819–81], 'What Rules the World', 1865*

Children begin by loving their parents. After a time they judge them. Rarely, if ever, do they forgive them.

Irish playwright and wit **Oscar Wilde** *[1854–1900],*
A Woman of No Importance, 1893

Fathers should neither be seen nor heard. That is the only proper basis for family life.

Irish playwright and wit **Oscar Wilde** *[1854–1900], in*
An Ideal Husband, 1899

To lose one parent, Mr Worthing, may be regarded as a misfortune; to lose both looks like carelessness.

Irish playwright and wit **Oscar Wilde** *[1854–1900],*
The Importance of Being Earnest, Act 1, 1895, Lady
Bracknell speaking

Before I got married I had six theories about bringing up children; now I have six children, and no theories.

Poet and courtier the second **Earl of Winchester**
[1647–80]

Till society is very differently constituted, parents, I fear, will still insist on being obeyed because they will be obeyed, and constantly endeavour to settle that power on a divine right which will not bear the investigation of reason . . . A slavish bondage to parents cramps every faculty of the mind.

Feminist writer **Mary Wollstonecraft** *[1759–97],*
A Vindication of the Rights of Women, Chapter 11, 1792

Dead! . . . and never called me mother!
Novelist **Mrs Henry Wood** *[1814–87], East Lynne,*
1861; the words do not appear in the novel, but were
inserted into one of its several stage versions

17

Family and friends

Friends are God's apology for relations.
> *Poet and critic* **Hugh Kingsmill** *[1889–1949],
> in Michael Holroyd, The Best of Hugh Kingsmill, 1970*

The close connection between the idea of family and the idea of friends goes back deep into the roots of our language: in the proverbial phrase 'kith and kin', for example, 'kith' means 'friends' – and even the word 'friend' itself derives from the Old Norse word for 'kinsman' (*frændi*). I find it a comforting thought – the tightly clenched phalanx of siblings and kinsmen, flanked by friends who themselves are frequently thought of as 'family friends'. Friendship can be every bit as complex a relationship as a family relationship, sometimes indistinguishably so, just as love can be. The Old Testament story of David and Jonathan in 1 Samuel has made them a synonym for intense and unbreakable friendship – but that friendship was also intertwined with intimate family relationships (Jonathan was David's brother-in-law). The death of an old friend can be as desolating as the death of a near relation, or even more so. 'Family first' may well be one's motto, but friends are always there or thereabouts.

66 99

Friends are born, not made.
> *American historian and man of letters* **Henry Brooks Adams** *[1838–1918], The Education of Henry Adams, 1907*

A friend in power is a friend lost.
> *American historian and man of letters* **Henry Brooks Adams** *[1838–1918], The Education of Henry Adams, 1907*

One friend in a lifetime is much; two are many; three are hardly possible. Friendship needs a certain parallelism of life, a community of thought, a rivalry of aim.
> *American historian and man of letters* **Henry Brooks Adams** *[1838–1918], The Education of Henry Adams, 1907*

Family is the ballast which stops you floating away, rudderless and anchorless.
> **Anon**

Count your age with friends but not with years.
> **Anon**

215

I may be wrong, but I have never found that deserting friends conciliates enemies.

Scottish political hostess and writer **Margot Asquith**
[1864–1945], Lay Sermons, 1927

Nobody who has not been in the interior of a family can say what the difficulties of any individual of that family may be.

Novelist **Jane Austen** *[1775–1817], Emma, 1815*

Friendship is certainly the finest balm for the pangs of disappointed love.

Novelist **Jane Austen** *[1775–1817], Northanger Abbey, 1818*

A false friend is more dangerous than an open enemy.

Courtier and philosopher **Francis Bacon** *[Lord Verulam, 1561–1626], A Letter of Advice to the Duke of Buckingham, 1605*

The worst families are those in which the members never really speak their minds to one another; they maintain an atmosphere of unreality, and everyone always lives in an atmosphere of suppressed ill-will.

Constitutional historian **Walter Bagehot** *[1826–77], The English Constitution, Introduction, 1867*

It may be more difficult to make new friends as you get older but it is some consolation to know how easy it is to lose them when you are young.

Journalist **Jeffrey Bernard** *[1932–97], in the Spectator,*
17 August 1985

A faithful friend is the medicine of life.

Bible, *Apocrypha, Ecclesiasticus 6:16*

Friendship, *n*. A ship big enough to carry two in fair weather, but only one in foul.

American journalist **Ambrose Bierce** *[1842–?1914],*
The Devil's Dictionary, 1906

The heart may think it knows better: the senses know that absence blots people out. We have really no absent friends.

Anglo–Irish novelist and short-story writer **Elizabeth Bowen** *[1891–1973], Death of the Heart, 1938*

Because I don't trust him, we are friends.

German dramatist and poet **Bertolt Brecht** *[1898–1956], Mother Courage, 1939*

Love is like the wild rose-briar,
Friendship like the holly-tree,
The holly is dark when the rose-briar blooms
But which will bloom most constantly?

Novelist **Emily Brontë** *[1818–48],*
'Love and Friendship', 1839

217

I believe that more unhappiness comes from this source (the family) than from any other – I mean from the attempt to prolong family connections unduly and to make people hang together artificially who would never naturally do so.

Writer **Samuel Butler** *[1835–1902], 'Elementary Morality', in The Note-Books of Samuel Butler, 1912*

Friendship is Love without his wings!

Poet **George, Lord Byron** *[1788–1824], 'L'Amitié est L'Amour sans Ailes', 1806*

Don't walk behind me, I may not lead. Don't walk in front of me, I may not follow. Just walk beside me and be my friend.

Attributed to French novelist **Albert Camus** *[1913–60]*

You can make more friends in two months by becoming interested in other people than you can in two years by trying to get other people interested in you.

American writer on self-improvement **Dale Carnegie** *[1888–1955], How to Win Friends and Influence People, 1936*

My true friends have always given me that supreme proof of devotion, a spontaneous aversion for the man I loved.

French novelist **Colette** *[Sidonie-Gabrielle Colette, 1873–1954], Break of Day, 1928*

The firmest friendships have been formed in mutual adversity, as iron is most strongly united by the fiercest flame.
Clergyman and writer **Charles Caleb Colton**
[c. 1780–1832], Lacon, 1825

It is a melancholy truth that even great men have their poor relations.
Novelist **Charles Dickens** *[1812–70], Bleak House, 1853*

Accidents will occur in the best-regulated families.
Novelist **Charles Dickens** *[1812–70], David Copperfield, 1850, Mr Micawber speaking*

To find a friend one must close one eye. To keep him – two.
Austrian-born Scottish writer **Norman Douglas**
[1868–1952], Almanac, 1941

There is no vocabulary
For love within a family, love that's lived in
But not looked at, love within the light of which
All else is seen, the light within which
All other love finds speech.
This love is silent.
American-born poet and playwright **T S Eliot**
[1888–1965], The Elder Statesman, 1958

A friend may well be reckoned the masterpiece of Nature.
American poet and essayist **Ralph Waldo Emerson**
[1803–82], 'Friendship', in Essays: First Series, 1841

It is in the thirties that we want friends. In the forties we know they won't save us any more than love did.

American novelist **F Scott Fitzgerald** *[1896–1940],*
'The Crack-Up', in Note-Books, 1945

If I had to choose between betraying my country and betraying my friend, I hope I should have the guts to betray my country.

Novelist **E M Forster** *[1879–1970], 'What I Believe',*
in Two Cheers for Democracy, 1951

The awe and dread with which the untutored savage contemplates his mother-in-law are amongst the most familiar facts of anthropology.

Scottish social anthropologist **James Frazer** *[1854–1941],*
The Golden Bough, 1900

The greatest thing in family life is to take a hint when a hint is intended – and not to take a hint when a hint isn't intended.

American poet **Robert Frost** *[1874–1963]*

A good friend is my nearest relation.

Writer and physician **Thomas Fuller** *[1654–1734],*
Gnomologia, 1732

You cannot shake hands with a clenched fist.

Attributed to Indian Prime Minister **Indira Gandhi**
[1917–80]

Families, I hate you! Shut-in homes, closed doors, jealous possessions of happiness.

French novelist **André Gide** *[1869–1951],*
Fruits of the Earth, 1897

We may be witnessing the first generation in history that has not been required to participate in that primal rite of socialisation, the family meal. The family meal is not only the core curriculum in the school of civilised discourse; it is also a set of protocols that curb our natural savagery and our animal greed, and cultivate a capacity for sharing and thoughtfulness.

Polish-born French writer **Francine du Plessix Gray**
[b. 1930], The New Yorker, October 1995

There's no need
to give a lot,
the price of praise can be cheap:
with half a loaf
and an empty cup
I found myself a friend.

Old Icelandic mythological poem **Hávamál**, *'The Words of*
the High One'

Natural affection is a prejudice: for though we have cause to love our nearest connections better than others, we have no reason to think them better than others.

Essayist **William Hazlitt** *[1778–1830], 'On Prejudice',*
in Sketches and Essays, published in 1839

Your friend is the man who knows all about you and still likes you.

> *American writer and editor* **Elbert Hubbard**
> *[1856–1915], The Note Book, 1927*

It has long been my belief that in times of great stress, such as a four-day vacation, the thin veneer of family wears off almost at once, and we are revealed in our true personalities.

> *American writer* **Shirley Jackson** *[1919–65], Raising Demons, 1956*

If a man does not make new acquaintances as he advances through life, he will soon find himself alone. A man, sir, should keep his friendships in good repair.

> *Writer and lexicographer* **Samuel Johnson** *[1709–84]*

The family you come from isn't as important as the family you're going to have.

> *American writer* **Ring Lardner** *[1885–1933]*

In the misfortunes of our closest friends, we always find something which is not displeasing to us.

> *French social reformer* **Duc de La Rochefoucauld-Llancourt** *[1747–1827], Maximes, 1665*

Far from being the basis of the good society, the family, with its narrow privacy and tawdry secrets, is the source of all our discontents.

> *Anthropologist* **Edmund Leach** *[1910–89], BBC Reith Lectures, 1967, The Listener, 30 November 1967*

A group of closely related persons living under one roof; it is a convenience, often a necessity, sometimes a pleasure, sometimes the reverse; but who first exalted it as admirable, an almost religious ideal?

Novelist **Rose Macaulay** *[1881–1958], The World My Wilderness, 1950*

It's no good trying to keep up old friendships. It's painful for both sides. The fact is, one grows out of people, and the only thing is to face it.

Novelist and short-story writer **W Somerset Maugham** *[1874–1965], Cakes and Ale, 1930*

A man of active and resilient mind outwears his friendships just as certainly as he outwears his love affairs, his politics and his epistemology.

American journalist and literary critic **H L Mencken** *[1880–1956], Prejudices: Third Series, 1922*

Money couldn't buy friends, but you got a better class of enemy.

Comedian **Spike Milligan** *[1918–2002], Puckoon, 1963*

> One would be in less danger
> From the wiles of a stranger
> If one's own kin and kith
> Were more fun to be with.

American poet **Ogden Nash** *[1902–71], 'Family Court', in Verses From 1929 On, 1959*

Love demands infinitely less than friendship.
> *American drama critic* **George Jean Nathan**
> *[1882–1958], 'Attitude towards Love and Marriage',*
> *in The Autobiography of an Attitude, 1925*

In a friend you find a second self.
> *French-born American writer* **Anaïs Nin** *[1903–77]*

Everybody knows how to raise children, except the people who have them.
> *American humorist* **P J O'Rourke** *[b. 1947], The Bachelor*
> *Home Companion, 1987*

A family is but too often a commonwealth of malignants.
> *Poet and essayist* **Alexander Pope** *[1688–1744],*
> *Thoughts on Various Subjects, 1717*

Oh how hideous it is
To see three generations of one house gathered together!
It is like an old tree with shoots,
And with some branches rotted and falling.
> *American poet* **Ezra Pound** *[1885–1972],*
> *'Commission', 1916*

Do not protect yourself by a fence, but rather by your friends.

> **Proverb** – *Czech*

A hedge between keeps friendship green.

> **Proverb** – *English*

Everyone's companion is no man's friend.

Proverb – *German*

When the character of a man is not clear to you, look at his friends.

Proverb – *Japanese*

An ounce of blood is worth more than a pound of friendship.

Proverb – *Spanish*

Friendship is constant in all other things,
Save in the office and affairs of love.
Playwright **William Shakespeare** *[1564–1616], Much Ado About Nothing, Act 2, Scene 1, Claudio speaking*

If it is abuse – why, one is always sure to hear of it from one damned good-natured friend or another!
Irish dramatist and politician **Richard Brinsley Sheridan** *[1751–1816], The Critic, 1779*

The family – that dear octopus from whose tentacles we never quite escape.
Novelist and playwright **Dodie Smith** *[1896–1990], in the play Dear Octopus, 1938*

I am a hoarder of two things: documents and trusted friends.
Scottish novelist **Muriel Spark** *[b. 1918], Curriculum Vitae, 1992*

A friend is a gift we give ourselves.
Scottish writer **Robert Louis Stevenson** *[1850–94]*

The Family! – the home of all social evils, a charitable institution for indolent women, a prison workshop for the slaving bread-winner and a hell for children.
Swedish playwright and novelist **August Strindberg**
[1849–1912], The Son of a Servant, 1886

If a man's character is to be abused, say what you will, there's nobody like a relation to do the business.
Novelist **William Makepeace Thackeray** *[1811–63],*
Vanity Fair, 1848

There is no such thing as Society. There are individual men and women, and there are families.
Conservative Prime Minister **Margaret Thatcher**
[b. 1925], in Woman's Own, 31 October 1987

Greater love hath no man than this, that he lay down his friends for his life.
Liberal politician **Jeremy Thorpe** *[b. 1929], comment in*
July 1962 on Harold Macmillan's sacking of many of his
Cabinet

All happy families resemble one another, but each unhappy family is unhappy in its own way.
Russian novelist **Leo Tolstoy** *[1828–1910], Anna*
Karenina, 1875–77, opening words

The proper office of a friend is to side with you when you are in the wrong. Nearly anybody will side with you when you are in the right.

American writer **Mark Twain** *[Samuel Langhorne Clemens, 1835–1910], Notebooks, 1935*

I do not believe that friends are necessarily the people you like best, they are merely the people who got there first.

Russian-born actor and writer **Peter Ustinov** *[1921–2004], Dear Me, 1977*

Whenever a friend succeeds, a little something in me dies.

American novelist and critic **Gore Vidal** *[b. 1925], in Sunday Times Magazine, 16 September 1973*

I always like to know everything about my new friends, and nothing about my old friends.

Irish playwright and wit **Oscar Wilde** *[1854–1900]*

After a good dinner one can forgive anybody, even one's own relations.

Irish playwright and wit **Oscar Wilde** *[1854–1900], A Woman of No Importance, 1893*

It is no use telling me that there are bad aunts and good aunts. At the core, they are all alike. Sooner or later, out pops the cloven hoof.

Novelist **P G Wodehouse** *[1881–1975], The Code of the Woosters, 1938*

Think where man's glory most begins and ends
And say my glory was I had such friends.

Irish poet **William Butler Yeats** *[1865–1939],*
'The Municipal Gallery Re-visited', 1939

18

Middle age

The forties are the old age of youth; the fifties are the youth of old age. (**Proverb** – Polish)

Why do people seem to find middle age a bit of a joke or, at least, something to joke about? Men having a (self-induced?) midlife crisis, women hormonally and embarrassingly afflicted by the menopause – there is nothing inherently funny about either of them. It's a time of significant change – the time when you really begin to feel the process of ageing affecting your body, when blithe faith in your immortality is replaced by a disconcerting awareness of your mortality. No, it's nothing to laugh about, but we do, yes we do.

66 99

Years ago we discovered the exact point, the dead center of middle age. It occurs when you are too young to take up golf and too old to rush up to the net.

American journalist and humorist **Franklin P Adams**
[1881–1960], Nods and Becks, 1944

The Indian Summer of life should be a little sunny and a little sad, like the season, and infinite in wealth and depth of tone – but never hustled.

American historian and man of letters **Henry Brooks Adams** *[1838–1918], The Education of Henry Adams, 1907*

If you want to know how old a woman is, ask her sister-in-law.

American film director and actor **Woody Allen** *[b. 1935]*

> Sing hey diddle diddle,
> A middle-aged fiddle
> Can still play a jolly good tune;
> And always remember
> A rose in December
> Is a great deal more fun than in June.

Anon

Middle age is not the first time you can't do it twice, but the second time you can't do it once.

Anon

Middle age is when you try all night to do what you once did all night.

Anon

Middle age is when you can still do everything you always could, but don't feel like it.

Anon

Middle age is when you want to see how long your car will last instead of how fast it will go.

Anon

Except for an occasional heart attack I feel as young as I ever did.

American humorous writer **Robert Benchley**
[1889–1945]

You are thirty-two. You are rapidly approaching the age when your body, whether it embarrasses you or not, begins to embarrass other people.

Playwright and actor **Alan Bennett** *[b. 1934],*
Getting On, 1972

Middle age is having a choice between two temptations and choosing the one that'll get you home earlier.

American columnist **Dan Bennett**

Middle age is a dispiritingly practical age. There is a tendency to sift through unfulfilled dreams and begin chucking out the wilder ones.

> *Humorist and columnist* **Alan Coren** *[b. 1938],*
> *Seems Like Old Times, 1989*

When a middle-aged man says in a moment of weariness that he is half dead, he is telling the literal truth.

> *American columnist and radio commentator* **Elmer Holmes Davis** *[1890–1958], 'On Not Being Dead, As Reported', in By Elmer Davis, published in 1964*

The really frightening thing about middle age is the knowledge that you'll grow out of it.

> *American actress* **Doris Day** *[b. 1924]*

The years between fifty and seventy are the hardest. You are always being asked to do things and yet you are not decrepit enough to turn them down.

> *American-born poet and playwright* **T S Eliot** *[1888–1965], in an interview in Time magazine, 23 October 1950*

Home is where one starts from. As we grow older
The world becomes stranger, the pattern more complicated
Of dead and living.

> *American-born poet and playwright* **T S Eliot** *[1888–1965], 'East Coker', in Four Quartets, 1940*

As you get older, the pickings get slimmer but the people don't.

American actress **Carrie Fisher** *[b. 1956]*

Whoever, in middle age, attempts to realise the wishes and hopes of his early youth, invariably deceives himself. Each ten years of a man's life has its own fortunes, its own hopes, its own desires.

German poet **Johann Wolfgang von Goethe**
[1749–1832], Elective Affinities, 1809

As you got older, and felt yourself to be at the centre of your time, and not at a point in its circumference, as you felt when you were little, you were seized with a sort of shuddering.

Novelist and poet **Thomas Hardy** *[1840–1928],*
Jude the Obscure, 1895

Men, like peaches and pears, grow sweet a little while before they begin to decay.

American physician and writer **Oliver Wendell Holmes,**
Sr *[1809–94], The Autocrat of the Breakfast Table, 1858*

Middle age is when your age starts to show around your middle.

American comedian **Bob Hope** *[1903–2003], interview,*
15 February 1954

233

When summer's end is nighing
And skies at evening cloud,
I muse on change and fortune
And all the feats I vowed
When I was young and proud.

Poet **A E Housman** *[1859–1936], Last Poems, No. 39,*
1922

Nature is as wasteful of promising young men as she is
of fish-spawn. It's not just getting them killed in wars:
mere middle age snuffs out ten times more talent than
ever wars and sudden death do.

Welsh-born writer **Richard Hughes** *[1900–76], The Fox*
in the Attic, Book I, 1961

I think middle age is the best time, if we can escape the
fatty degeneration of the conscience which often sets in
at about fifty.

Writer and Dean of St Paul's **William R Inge**
[1860–1954], quoted in the Observer, 8 June 1930

Whenever a man's friends begin to compliment him
about looking young, he may be sure that they think he
is growing old.

American writer **Washington Irving** *[1783–1859],*
'Bachelors', in Bracebridge Hall, 1822

Men at forty
Learn to close softly
The doors to rooms they will not be
Coming back to.

American poet **Donald Justice** *[b. 1925], 'Men at Forty',*
1967

By the time a man notices that he is no longer young, his youth has long since left him.

French novelist and playwright **François Mauriac**
[1885–1970], 'The Age of Success', in Second Thoughts,
1961

What a pity it is that there is so little space between the time when one is young and the time when one becomes old.

French philosopher **Charles, Baron de Montesquieu**
[1689–1755]

Middle age is when you are sitting at home on a Saturday night and the telephone rings and you hope it isn't for you.

American poet **Ogden Nash** *[1902–71]*

Middle age is when you have met so many people that every new person you meet reminds you of someone else – and usually is.

American poet **Ogden Nash** *[1902–71], 'Let's Not Climb*
the Washington Monument Tonight', in Versus, 1949

I have a bone to pick with Fate.
Come here and tell me, girlie,
Do you think my mind is maturing late,
Or simply rotted early?
American poet **Ogden Nash** *[1902–71], 'Lines on Facing Forty'*

Middle-aged life is merry, and I love to lead it.
American poet **Ogden Nash** *[1902–71], Peekaboo, I Almost See You*

The Americans are now labeling middle age as the Command Generation: 'We are the generations who have been active and vociferous about the right to be who and what we are' … Yet, far from feeling in command, many of us find ourselves feeling chronologically dispossessed, too old to be called young any longer and too young to be called old. It feels like an important time, but it is afforded no importance. As I see it, we have a choice between ignoring midlife and hoping it doesn't really exist, and embracing it, turning it into a particularly valuable time of assessment and preparation.
Journalist **Angela Neustatter**, *Look the Demon in the Eye, 1996*

Age is a question of mind over matter. If you don't mind, it doesn't matter.
Attributed to American baseball player **Leroy 'Satchel' Paige** *[1906–82] and various others*

Middle age is when anything new in the way you feel is most likely a symptom.

Canadian writer **Laurence J Peter** *[1919–90]*

From forty to fifty a man is at heart either a stoic or a satyr.

Playwright **Arthur Wing Pinero** *[1855–1934],*
The Second Mrs Tanqueray, Act 1, 1893

One of the pleasures of middle age is to *find out* that one WAS right, and that one was much righter than one knew at say 17 or 23.

American poet **Ezra Pound** *[1885–1972],*
ABC of Reading, 1934

As we get older we do not get any younger.
Seasons return, and today I am fifty-five,
And this time last year I was fifty-four,
And this time next year I shall be sixty-two.

Poet and playwright **Henry Reed** *[1914–86], 'Chard*
Whitlow', A Map of Verona, 1946, in parody of T S Eliot

The first forty years of life are the text, the rest is the commentary.

German philosopher **Arthur Schopenhauer** *[1788–1860]*

Just remember, once you're over the hill you begin to pick up speed.

American cartoonist **Charles M Schulz** *[1922–2000],*
'Peanuts'

On his bold visage middle age
Had slightly press'd its signet sage,
Yet had not quench'd the open truth
And fiery vehemence of youth.
Scottish novelist and poet **Sir Walter Scott** *[1771–1823],*
The Lady of the Lake, 1810

Every man over forty is a scoundrel.
Irish playwright and critic **George Bernard Shaw**
[1856–1950], Maxims for Revolutionaries, prologue to
Man and Superman

There is more felicity on the far side of baldness than young men can possibly imagine.
American-born British writer **Logan Pearsall Smith**
[1865–1946], Afterthoughts, 1931

Age is a high price to pay for maturity.
Playwright **Tom Stoppard** *[b. 1937], Where Are They*
Now?, 1973

Every twenty years the middle-aged celebrate the decade of their youth.
American novelist and critic **Gore Vidal** *[b. 1925], in the*
Observer Review, 27 August 1989

In a man's middle years there is scarcely a part of the body he would hesitate to turn over to the proper authorities.
American humorist **E B White** *[1899–1985], 'A Weekend*
with the Angels', in The Second Tree from the Corner, 1954

Thirty-five is a very attractive age. London society is full of women of the very highest birth who have, of their own free choice, remained thirty-five for years.

Irish playwright and wit **Oscar Wilde** *[1854–1900],*
The Importance of Being Earnest, 1895

Be wise with speed:
A fool at forty is a fool indeed.
Poet and clergyman **Edward Young** *[1683–1765]*

19
Old age

To me, old age is always fifteen years older than I am.
(American businessman and political sage
Bernard Baruch [1870–1965], said on his
eighty-fifth birthday)

I was born in October 1929; I reckon that qualifies me as being
'old'. It certainly gives a keen edge to my selection of citations
about old age – what it feels like, what it looks like, all the
intimations of approaching mortality. Old age has its hopes as
well as its despairs, however, and I find most of these quotations curiously comforting, and many of them very illumina-
ting. Or am I just kidding myself?

❝❞

To keep the heart unwrinkled, to be hopeful, kindly, cheerful, reverent – that is to triumph over old age.

> *American novelist and playwright* **Thomas Bailey Aldrich** *[1836–1907], 'Leaves from a Notebook', in Ponkapog Papers, 1903*

I recently turned sixty. Practically a third of my life is over.

> *American film director and actor* **Woody Allen** *[b. 1935]*

There are no pleasures in life worth forgoing in return for two more years in a nursing-home in Weston-Super-Mare.

> *Novelist and critic* **Kingsley Amis** *[1922–95]*

The older I get, the better I used to be.

> **Anon**, *attributed to some former athlete*

If I had known I was going to live so long I would have taken better care of myself.

> **Anon**, *attributed to several old troupers*

Old age is not a disease. Because a person is old, he is not inadequate. There is youth in old age, and beauty too, if we only have eyes to see.

> **Anon**

It's sad for a girl to reach the age
Where men consider her charmless,
But it's worse for a man to attain the age
Where girls consider him harmless.

> **Anon**

The late Queen Mother was visiting a geriatric home. As she was doing her rounds she leaned over towards one old lady sitting there, and said brightly, 'Good morning.' The old lady looked a bit puzzled, so the Queen Mother said, 'Do you know who I am?' Whereupon the old lady gave her a sympathetic look and said, 'No, dear, but if you ask the matron, she'll tell you.'

Anon

Old age and treachery will always triumph over youth and skill.

Anon

The toothless self-absorption of old age.

Anon

Man is not old when his hair turns grey,
Man is not old when his teeth decay,
But man is approaching his long last sleep
When his mind makes appointments his body cannot
  keep.

Anon

Growing old is mandatory. Growing up is optional.

Anon

You know you're growing old when:
Your knees buckle and your belt won't;
You regret all the temptations you resisted;

You simply can't stand people who are intolerant;
You burn the midnight oil until 9 p.m.;
You sink your teeth into a steak and they stay there.

Anon

Education is the best provision for old age.
Greek philosopher **Aristotle** *[384–322 BC]*

It is – last stage of all –
When we are frozen up within, and quite
The phantom of ourselves,
To hear the world applaud the hollow ghost
Which blamed the living man.
Poet and essayist **Matthew Arnold** *[1822–88],
'Growing Old', in New Poems, 1867*

All I have to live on now is macaroni and memorial services.
Scottish political hostess and writer **Margot Asquith**
*[1864–1945], quoted in Chips Cannon's diary,
16 September 1943*

Old age is like everything else – to make a success of it,
you have to start young.
American actor and dancer **Fred Astaire** *[1899–1987]*

In England, you see, age wipes the slate clean . . . If you
live to be ninety in England and can still eat a boiled
egg, they think you deserve the Nobel Prize.
Playwright and actor **Alan Bennett** *[b. 1934], An
Englishman Abroad, 1989*

With the ancient is wisdom; and in length of days understanding.

Bible, *Job 12:12*

They shall grow not old, as we that are left grow old:
Age shall not weary them, nor the years condemn.
At the going down of the sun and in the morning
We will remember them.

Poet **Laurence Binyon** *[1869–1943], 'For the Fallen',*
1914

Old age is . . . a lot of crossed-off names in an address
book.

Writer **Ronald Blythe** *[b. 1922]*

Grow old along with me!
The best is yet to be,
The last of life, for which the first was made.

Poet **Robert Browning** *[1812–89], 'Rabbi Ben Ezra',*
in Dramatis Personae, 1864

First you forget names, then you forget faces. Next you
forget to pull your zipper up and finally you forget to
pull it down.

American comedian **George Burns** *[1896–1996]*

When asked at the age of ninety-three what sex was like,
American comedian **George Burns** *[1896–1996]* replied:
'It's like playing billiards with a rope.'

The gardener's rule applies to youth and age:
When young, sow wild oats; but when old, grow sage.
Playwright and actor **H J Byron** *[1834–84], 'An Adage'*

As a white candle
In a holy place,
So is the beauty
Of an aged face.
Irish poet **Joseph Campbell** *[1879–1944],*
'The Old Woman'

You don't let old age happen to you, you happen to it.
Labour politician **Barbara Castle** *[1910–2002], quoted*
by Angela Neustatter in Look the Demon in the Eye, 1996

Growing old isn't so bad when you consider the alternative.
French entertainer **Maurice Chevalier** *[1888–1972],*
on his seventy-second birthday, New York Times,
9 October 1960

No one is so old that he does not think he could live another year.
Roman orator and statesman **Cicero** *[106–43 BC],*
De Senectute, 44 BC

I have never felt that the contemplation of the past, with the knowledge that it cannot come again, need be a source of sorrow. The emotion is like that aroused by looking through an album of old photographs which recall happy days, and if we find among them the faces of friends who are no more we are glad to be reminded of the affection we felt for them. I have written this book, and enjoyed writing it, because I wanted to set down some of these memories before they faded. Nor can the dearest and the most sacred of them be included. Life has been good to me and I am grateful. My delight in it is as keen as ever and I will thankfully accept as many more years as may be granted. But I am fond of change and have welcomed it even when uncertain whether it would be for the better; so, although I am very glad to be where I am, I should not be too distressed when the summons comes to go away. Autumn has always been my favourite season, and eventide has been for me the pleasantest time of day. I love the sun light but I cannot fear the coming of the dark.

Conservative politician and diplomat **Duff Cooper**
[First Viscount Norwich, 1890–1954], Old Men Forget,
1953

Regrets are the natural property of grey hairs.
Novelist **Charles Dickens** *[1812–70],*
Martin Chuzzlewit, 1844

When a man fell into his anecdotage it was a sign for him to retire from the world.
Tory Prime Minister and novelist **Benjamin Disraeli**
[1804–81], Lothair, 1870

No spring, nor summer beauty hath such grace,
As I have seen in one autumnal face.

Poet and divine **John Donne** *[1572–1631],
'The Autumnal', Elegy 9, 1634*

Within, I do not find wrinkles and used heart, but unspent youth.

American poet and essayist **Ralph Waldo Emerson**
[1803–82], Journals, 1864

The first imperative for those wishing to be a healthy hundred is to be informed, stay in command, and be thoroughly obstreperous in refusing to be fobbed off with second-rate medical care.

John Grimley Evans, *Professor of Clinical Gerontology
at Oxford University, interviewed in The Times,
17 October 1995*

Older women are best because they always think they may be doing it for the last time.

Novelist **Ian Fleming** *[1908–64], quoted in
John Pearson, The Life of Ian Fleming, 1966*

Anyone who stops learning is old, whether at twenty or eighty. Anyone who keeps learning stays young. The greatest thing in life is to keep your mind young.

American industrialist **Henry Ford** *[1863–1947]*

All would live long, but none would be old.
> *American politician and scientist* **Benjamin Franklin**
> *[1706–90]*

I don't need you to remind me of my age, I have a bladder to do that for me.
> *Actor and writer* **Stephen Fry** *[b. 1957], Paperweight,*
> *1992*

In old age, the consolation of hope is reserved for the tenderness of parents, who commence a new life in their children; the faith of enthusiasts, who sing Hallelujahs above the clouds; and the vanity of authors who presume the immortality of their names and writings.
> *Historian* **Edward Gibbon** *[1737–94], last sentence of*
> *his Autobiography*

I love everything that's old: old friends, old times, old manners, old books, old wines; and I believe, Dorothy, you'll own I have been pretty fond of an old wife.
> *Irish-born writer and playwright* **Oliver Goldsmith**
> *[1730–74], in She Stoops to Conquer, Act 1, Scene 1,*
> *1773, Hardcastle speaking to his wife*

There comes a time when it is too late to retire.
> *Attributed to Conservative politician* **Lord Hailsham**
> *[1907–2001] by journalist Ted Pickering on his own*
> *ninetieth birthday party, 3 May 2002*

If you rest, you rust.

American actress **Helen Hayes** *[1900–93], at the age of*
eighty-eight

It may be made a question whether men grow wiser as they grow older, any more than they grow stronger or healthier or honester.

Essayist **William Hazlitt** *[1778–1830],*
'On Knowledge of the World', in Sketches and Essays,
published in 1839

To be seventy years young is sometimes far more cheerful and hopeful than to be forty years old.

American jurist **Oliver Wendell Holmes Jr**
[1841–1935]

To my deafness I'm accustomed,
To my dentures I'm resigned,
I can manage my bifocals,
But O, how I miss my mind.

Conservative Prime Minister **Alex Douglas Home**
[1903–95]

You know you're getting old when the candles cost more than the cake.

American comedian **Bob Hope** *[1903–2003]*

Jenny kiss'd me when we met,
Jumping from the chair she sat in;
Time, you thief, who love to get
Sweets into your list, put that in:
Say I'm weary, say I'm sad,
Say that health and wealth have miss'd me;
Say I'm growing old, but add,
Jenny kissed me.

Poet and literary critic **Leigh Hunt** *[1784–1859],*
'Rondeau', 1838

Age is a question of mind over matter. If you don't mind,
it doesn't matter.

American jazz musician **Dan Ingman**

No man is ever old enough to know better.

Journalist and editor **Holbrook Jackson** *[1874–1948]*

When I am an old woman I shall wear purple
With a red hat which doesn't go, and doesn't suit me,
And I shall spend my pension on brandy and summer
 gloves
And satin sandals, and say we've no money for butter.

Poet **Jenny Joseph** *[b. 1932], 'Warning' in New Poems,*
a PEN anthology, 1965

I warmed both hands before the fire of life;
It sinks, and I am ready to depart.
Poet and writer **Walter Savage Landor** *[1775–1864],*
'Dying Speech of an Old Philosopher', 1849

Old men like to give good advice in order to console
themselves for not being able to set bad examples.
French social reformer **Duc de La Rochefoucauld-**
Llancourt *[1613–80], Maximes, 1665*

Grand Old Man: that means on our continent anyone
with snow-white hair who has kept out of jail till eighty.
Canadian economist and humorist **Stephen Leacock**
[1869–1944], Three Score and Ten

Age is not a particularly interesting subject. Anyone can
get old. All you have to do is live long enough.
American comedian **Groucho Marx** *[1895–1977],*
Groucho and Me, 1959

They say a man is as old as the women he feels. In that
case, I'm eighty-five.
American comedian **Groucho Marx** *[1895–1977],*
The Secret Word is Groucho, 1976

There comes a time in every man's life when he must
make way for an older man.
Conservative politician **Reginald Maudling** *[1917–77],*
on being replaced in the Shadow Cabinet by a man four years
his senior: reported in the Guardian, 20 September 1976

Old age has its pleasures which, though different, are not less than the pleasures of youth.

Novelist and short-story writer **W Somerset Maugham**
[1874–1965], The Summing Up, 1938

I am sick of this way of life. The weariness and sadness of old age make it intolerable. I have walked with death in hand, and death's own hand is warmer than my own. I don't wish to live any longer.

Novelist and short-story writer **W Somerset Maugham**
[1874–1965], interviewed on his ninetieth birthday

Old age is like a plane flying through a storm. Once you are aboard there is nothing you can do about it.

Israeli Prime Minister **Golda Meir** *[1898–1978],*
at the age of seventy-five

What lips my lips have kissed, and where, and why,
I have forgotten, and what arms have lain
Under my head till morning; but the rain
Is full of ghosts tonight, that tap and sigh
Upon the glass and listen for reply;
And in my heart there stirs a quiet pain
For unremembered lads that not again
Will turn to me at midnight with a cry.
Thus in the winter stands the lonely tree,
Nor knows what birds have vanished one by one,
Yet knows its boughs more silent than before:
I cannot say what loves have come and gone;

I only know that summer sang in me
A little while, that in me sings no more.
American poet **Edna St Vincent Millay** *[1892–1950],*
'What Lips My Lips Have Kissed, and Where, and Why'

When you get to my age life seems little more than one
long march to and from the lavatory.
Novelist and playwright **John Mortimer** *[b. 1923]*

Senescence begins
And middle age ends
The day your descendants
Outnumber your friends.
American poet **Ogden Nash** *[1902–71], 'Crossing the*
Boarder', in Marriage Lines, 1964

There's one more terrifying fact about old people: I'm
going to be one soon.
American humorist **P J O'Rourke** *[b. 1947], Parliament*
of Whores, 1991

Growing old is like being increasingly penalised for a
crime you haven't committed.
Novelist **Anthony Powell** *[1905–2000], Temporary*
Kings, 1973

Everything comes about just as we desired, but only
when we no longer desire it.
French novelist **Marcel Proust** *[1871–1922],*
Remembrance of Things Past

Age is a bad travelling companion.

Proverb – *English*

An old man loved is winter with flowers.

Proverb – *German*

Deeds for the young, counsels for the middle-aged, prayers for the old.

Proverb – *Greek*

The greatest cultural achievement of a society is a contented older generation.

Proverb – *Japanese*

Youth feeds on dreams, old age on memories.

Proverb – *Jewish*

If you would grow old, you must start early.

Proverb – *Spanish*

Ancient Person, for whom I
All the flattering Youth defy,
Long be it ere thou grow Old,
Aching, shaking, crazy Cold;
But still continue as thou art,
Ancient Person of my Heart.

On thy wither'd Lips and Dry,
Which like barren Furrows lye,
Brooding Kisses I will pour

Shall thy Youthful Heat restore
(Such kind show'rs in Autumn fall,
And a Second Spring recall);
Nor from thee will ever part,
Ancient Person of my Heart.

Thy Nobler parts, which but to name
In our sex would be counted shame,
By Age's frozen grasp possest,
From their ice shall be releast,
And sooth'd by my reviving hand
In former warmth and vigour stand.

All a lover's wish can reach
For thy Joy my love shall teach,
And for thy Pleasure shall improve
All that Art can add to Love.
Yet still I love thee without Art,
Ancient Person of my Heart.

Courtier and poet **John Wilmot, Earl of Rochester**
[1647–80], 'A Song of a Young Lady to her Ancient Lover'

The young have aspirations that never come to pass, the
old have reminiscences of what never happened.
Scottish writer **Saki** *[H H Munro, 1870–1916], 'Reginald
at the Carlton', in Reginald, 1904*

As I grow older and older
And totter towards the tomb,
I find that I care less and less
Who goes to bed with whom.
Detective fiction writer **Dorothy L Sayers** *[1893–1957]*

Last scene of all,
That ends this strange eventful history,
Is second childishness and mere oblivion,
Sans teeth, sans eyes, sans taste, sans everything.
Playwright **William Shakespeare** *[1564–1616],*
As You Like It, Act 2, Scene 7, 1599–1600, the end of
Jaques' 'All the world's a stage' speech

Old men forget; yet all shall be forgot,
But he'll remember with advantages
What feats he did that day.
Playwright **William Shakespeare** *[1564–1616],*
King Henry V, Act 4, Scene 3

The oldest hath borne most: we that are young,
Shall never see so much, nor live so long.
Playwright **William Shakespeare** *[1564–1616],*
King Lear, final couplet, spoken by the Duke of Albany

Old people are dangerous, they have no fear of the future.
Irish playwright and critic **George Bernard Shaw**
[1856–1950]

One is born an incendiary and dies a fireman.
Irish playwright and critic **George Bernard Shaw**
[1856–1950]

We don't stop playing because we grow old, we grow old because we stop playing.
Attributed to Irish playwright and critic **George Bernard Shaw** *[1856–1950]*

The denunciation of the young is a necessary part of the hygiene of older people, and greatly assists the circulation of their blood.
American-born British writer **Logan Pearsall Smith** *[1865–1946], Last Words, 1933*

It's not the years in a life that count; it's the life in the years.
American Democratic statesman **Adlai Stevenson** *[1900–65]*

I have no room for new ideas.
Anglo-Irish writer and clergyman **Jonathan Swift** *[1667–1745], in advanced old age.*

Old age is a poor, untidy thing.
Irish playwright **J M Synge** *[1871–1909]*

The greatest problem of old age is the fear that it may go on too long.
Historian **A J P Taylor** *[1906–90]*

Do not go gentle into that good night,
Old age should burn and rave at close of day;
Rage, rage against the dying of the light.
Welsh poet and writer **Dylan Thomas** *[1914–53],*
'Do Not Go Gentle into that Good Night', 1952

The gods bestowed on Max (*Beerbohm*) the gift of perpetual old age.
Irish playwright and wit **Oscar Wilde** *[1854–1900],*
quoted in Aspects of Wilde by Vincent O'Sullivan, 1936

An aged man is but a paltry thing,
A tattered coat upon a stick, unless
Soul clap its hands and sing, and louder sing
For every tatter in its mortal dress.
Irish poet **William Butler Yeats** *[1835–1918], 'Sailing to*
Byzantium', 1927

20

Death

Death does not blow a trumpet. (**Proverb** – Danish)

We are at the ultimate chapter, the last boundary, the threshold of eternity, the end of the story of life. Some of us are closer to it than others; we only know for certain that it will come to all of us, sooner or later. How and when it comes, how we deal with it, how those who survive us cope with it – these are the piercing questions which have constantly exercised the human mind; consolation is expressed in philosophy or poetry or mordant humour, in bitter grief or peaceful resignation or stoic dignity. This is where all the quotations of life meet and seek resolution. Little wonder that this final bouquet in my anthology of quotations should be the most luxuriant one.

❝❞

When I read the several dates of the tombs, of some that died yesterday and some six hundred years ago, I consider that great day when we shall all of us be contemporaries, and make our appearance together.

Essayist and politician **Joseph Addison** *[1672–1719]*,
Thoughts in Westminster Abbey

It's not that I'm afraid to die. I just don't want to be there when it happens.

American film director and actor **Woody Allen** *[b. 1937]*,
Death, 1975

A dying man needs to die, as a sleepy man needs to sleep, and there comes a time when it is wrong, as well as useless, to resist.

American journalist **Stewart Alsop** *[1914–74]*

You can shed tears that she is gone
or you can smile because she has lived.
You can close your eyes and pray that she'll come back
or you can open your eyes and see all that she's left.
Your heart can be empty because you can't see her
or you can be full of the love you shared.
You can turn your back on tomorrow and live yesterday
or you can be happy for tomorrow because of yesterday.
You can remember her and only that she's gone
or you can cherish her memory and let it live on.
You can try and close your mind, be empty and turn
    your back

or you can do what she'd want: smile, open your eyes,
love and go on.

Anon, *known familiarly as 'The Queen Mother Poem'*
after it was read at her funeral in Westminster Abbey on
9 April 2002

Tears may soothe the wounds they cannot heal.

Anon

In death we leave behind all that we have; we take with
us all that we are.

Anon

Do not stand at my grave and weep;
I am not there. I do not sleep.
I am a thousand winds that blow.
I am the diamond glints on snow.
I am the sunlight on ripened grain.
I am the gentle autumn's rain.
When you awaken in the morning's hush,
I am the swift uplifting rush
Of quiet birds in circled flight.
I am the soft stars that shine at night.
Do not stand at my grave and cry;
I am not there: I did not die.

Anon, *some think it is a Navajo burial prayer.*
It was broadcast on BBC TV's Bookworm programme on
Remembrance Sunday, 1995

Death is nature's way of telling you to slow down.

Anon

It isn't the cough that carries you off,
It's the coffin they carry you off in.

Anon

Death has to be waiting at the end of the ride before you truly see the earth, and feel your heart, and love the world.

French playwright **Jean Anouilh** *[1910–87], The Lark,
1955*

I do not believe that any man fears to be dead, but only the stroke of death.

Courtier and philosopher **Francis Bacon** *[Lord Verulam,
1561–1626], The Remaines of . . . Lord Verulam,
published in 1648*

To die will be an awfully big adventure.

Scottish playwright **J M Barrie** *[1860–1937], Peter Pan,
Act 3, 1928*

Every tiny part of us cries out against the idea of dying, and hopes to live forever.

Italian playwright and poet **Ugo Betti** *[1892–1953],
Struggle Till Dawn, 1949*

Dust thou art, and unto dust shalt thou return.

Bible, *Genesis 3:19*

We must needs die, and are as water spilt on the ground, which cannot be gathered up again.
                                 Bible, *2 Samuel 14:14*

The last enemy that shall be destroyed is death.
                                 Bible, *1 Corinthians 15:26*

On this side and on that, men see their friends
        Drop off like leaves in autumn.
Scottish clergyman and poet **Robert Blair** *[1699–1746]*,
                                 The Grave, 1743

Death is the supreme festival on the road to freedom.
        German Lutheran pastor **Dietrich Bonhoeffer**
[1906–45], *'Miscellaneous Thoughts', in Letters and
                        Papers from Prison, 1953*

When Death to either shall come, –
        I pray it be first to me.
Poet **Robert Bridges** *[1844–1930]*, *'When Death to
                        Either Shall Come'*

I lingered round them, under that benign sky: watched the moths fluttering among the hearth and harebells; listened to the soft wind breathing through the grass; and wondered how anyone could ever imagine unquiet slumbers for the sleepers in that quiet earth.
        Novelist **Emily Brontë** *[1818–48]*, *Wuthering Heights,
                        1847, the closing lines*

263

Blow out, you bugles, over the rich Dead!
There's none of these so lonely and poor of old,
But, dying, has made us rarer gifts than gold.
These laid the world away; poured out the red
Sweet wine of youth; gave up the years to be
Of work and joy, and that unhoped serene,
That men call age; and those that would have been,
Their sons, they gave, their immortality.
    Poet **Rupert Brooke** *[1887–1915], 'The Dead', 1914*

Euthanasia is a long, smooth-sounding word, and it conceals its danger as long, smooth words do, but the danger is there, nonetheless.
American novelist **Pearl S Buck** *[1892–1973], The Child*
Who Never Grew, 1950

When you have told anyone you have left him a legacy, the only decent thing to do is to die at once.
    Writer **Samuel Butler** *[1835–1902], cited in Festing*
Jones, Samuel Butler: A Memoir

To live in hearts we leave behind
Is not to die.
Scottish poet **Thomas Campbell** *[1777–1844], 'Hallowed*
Ground'

What did it matter where you lay, once you were dead? In a dirty sump or in a marble tower on top of a high hill? You were dead, you were sleeping the big sleep, you were not bothered by things like that. Oil and water were

the same as wind and air to you. You just slept the big
sleep, not caring about the nastiness of how you died or
where you fell.

American detective fiction writer **Raymond Chandler**
[1888–1959], The Big Sleep, 1939

Dear God: Instead of letting people die and having to
make new ones why don't you just keep the ones you got
now? Jane.

*From **Children's Letters to God**, Eric Marshall and
Stewart Hample, 1975*

> Some are afraid of Death.
> They run from him, and cry
> Aloud, shrinking with fear
> When he draws near.
> Others take their last breath
> As though it were a sigh
> Of sheer content, or bliss
> Beneath a lover's kiss.
> Perhaps it is not much,
> After life's labour,
> That summoning touch
> Of Death, our neighbour.

Poet **Richard Church** *[1893–1972], 'Two Ways'*

Pale death, the grand physician, cures all pain;
The dead rest well who lived for joys in vain.
Poet **John Clare** *['The Northamptonshire Peasant Poet',
1793–1864], 'Child Harold', 1841*

Thou shalt not kill; but need'st not strive
Officiously to keep alive.
Poet **Arthur Hugh Clough** *[1819–61], 'The Latest*
Decalogue', 1862

And when life's sweet fable ends,
Soul and body part like friends;
No quarrels, murmurs, no delay;
A kiss, a sigh, and so away.
Poet **Richard Crashaw** *[c. 1612–49], 'Temperance',*
1652

The Bustle in a House
The Morning after Death
Is solemnest of industries
Enacted upon Earth –
The sweeping up the Heart
And putting Love away
We shall not want to use again
Until Eternity.
American poet **Emily Dickinson** *[1830–86],*
'The Bustle in a House'

No man is an Island, entire of itself; every man is
a piece of the Continent, a part of the main; if a clod
be washed away by the sea, Europe is the less, as well
as if a promontory were, as well as if a manor of thy
friends or of thine own were; any man's death dim-
inishes me, because I am involved in Mankind. And

therefore never send to know for whom the bell tolls; it tolls for thee.

Poet and divine **John Donne** *[1572–1631], Devotions upon Emergent Occasions, 'Meditation XVII', 1624*

Death be not proud, though some have called thee
Mighty and dreadful, for thou are not so,
For, those, whom thou think'st, thou dost overthrow,
Die not, poor death, nor yet canst thou kill me.

Poet and divine **John Donne** *[1572–1631],
Holy Sonnets, No 6, 1609*

Timor mortis conturbat me. – Fear of death disturbeth me.

Scottish poet **William Dunbar** *[c. 1460–c. 1520],
'Lament for the Makars', the refrain*

The bodies of those that made such a noise and tumult when alive, when dead, lie as quietly among the graves of their neighbours as any others.

American theologian **Jonathan Edwards** *[1703–58],
Miscellaneous Discourses in Works, 1834*

It hath often been said, that it is not death, but dying, which is terrible.

Novelist and judge **Henry Fielding** *[1707–54], Amelia, 1751*

Plan for this world as if you expect to live forever; but plan for the hereafter as if you expect to die tomorrow.

Spanish Moorish poet **Solomon Ibn Gabirol**
[c. 1021–58]

Death is a grim creditor, and a doctor but brittle bail
when the hour o' reckoning's at han'!
Scottish novelist **John Galt** *[1779–1839], Annals of the*
Parish, 1821

Is life a boon?
If so, it must befall
That Death, whene'er he call,
Must call too soon.
Writer and librettist **W S Gilbert** *[1836–1911],*
The Yeoman of the Guard, Act 1, 1888, ballad sung by
Fairfax

I'm told he makes a very handsome corpse, and becomes
his coffin prodigiously.
Irish-born writer and playwright **Oliver Goldsmith**
[1730–74], The Good Natur'd Man, 1668

Few are wholly dead:
Blow on a dead man's embers
And a live flame will start.
Poet **Robert Graves** *[1895–1985], 'To Bring the Dead to*
Life'

The boast of heraldry, the pomp of pow'r,
And all that beauty, all that wealth e'er gave,
Awaits alike th' inevitable hour,
The paths of glory lead but to the grave.
Poet **Thomas Gray** *[1716–71], 'Elegy Written in a*
Country Churchyard', 1751

Death borders upon our birth, and our cradle stands in the grave.

> Clergyman and writer **Joseph Hall** *[1574–1656],*
> *Epistles, 1608*

> Cattle die, kinsfolk die;
> You yourself must one day die.
> But one thing I know never dies –
> Word-fame, if justly earned.
>
> Old Icelandic mythological poem **Hávamál**, *'Words of the*
> *High One'*

Death cancels everything but truth; and strips a man of everything but genius and virtue. It is a sort of natural canonisation.

> Essayist **William Hazlitt** *[1778–1830], 'Lord Byron',*
> *in The Spirit of the Age, 1825*

> So be my passing!
> My task accomplished and the long day done,
> My wages taken, and in my heart
> Some late lark singing,
> Let me be gathered to the quiet west
> The sundown splendid and serene,
> Death.
>
> Poet **W E Henley** *[1848–1903]*

Death is like an arrow which is already in flight, and your life lasts only until it reaches you.

> German theologian **Georg Hermes** *[1775–1831]*

Death is nothing at all. It does not count. I have only slipped away into the next room. Nothing has happened. Everything remains exactly as it was. I am I, and you are you, and the old life that we lived so fondly together is untouched, unchanged. Whatever we were to each other, that we are still. Call me by the old familiar name. Speak of me in the easy way which you always used. Put no difference into your tone. Wear no forced air of solemnity or sorrow. Laugh as we always laughed at the little jokes that we enjoyed together. Play, smile, think of me, pray for me. Let my name be ever the household word that it always was. Let it be spoken without an effort, without the ghost of a shadow upon it. Life means all that it ever meant. It is the same as it ever was. There is absolute and unbroken continuity. What is this death but a negligible accident? Why should I be out of mind because I am out of sight? I am but waiting for you, for an interval, somewhere very near, just around the corner. All is well. Nothing is hurt; nothing is lost. One brief moment and all will be as it was before. How we shall laugh at the trouble of parting when we meet again!

*Anglican clergyman and canon **Henry Scott Holland** [1847–1918], 'The King of Terrors', a sermon on death delivered in St Paul's Cathedral on Whitsunday 1910, while the body of King Edward VII was lying in state at Westminster: published in Facts of the Faith, 1919*

Most persons have died before they expire – died to all earthly longings, so that the last breath is only, as it were, the locking of the door of the already deserted mansion.
American physician and writer **Oliver Wendell Holmes, Sr** *[1809–94], The Professor at the Breakfast Table, 1860*

Here dead lie we because we did not choose
To live and shame the land from which we sprung.
Life, to be sure, is nothing much to lose;
But young men think it is, and we were young.
Poet **A E Housman** *[1859–1936]: inscribed on a plaque in the British War Cemetery on the island of Vis in the Adriatic*

It matters not how a man dies, but how he lives. The act of dying is not of importance, it lasts so short a time.
Critic and lexicographer **Samuel Johnson** *[1709–84], cited in James Boswell, Life of Samuel Johnson, 1791*

All life is trouble, it is only death that is no trouble.
Greek novelist **Nikos Kazantzakis** *[1883–1957], Zorba the Greek, 1946*

Sleep on (my Love!) in thy cold bed,
Never to be disquieted.
My last Good-night! Thou wilt not wake
Till I thy fate shall overtake:
Till age, or grief, or sickness must
Marry my body to that dust
It so much loves; and fill the room

My heart keeps empty in thy tomb.
Stay for me there: I will not fail
To meet thee in that hollow vale.
Poet and bishop **Henry King** *[1592–1669], 'An Exequy'*
(on his wife Anne), 1657

Gone before
To that unknown and silent shore.
Writer **Charles Lamb** *[1775–1834], 'Hester', 1803*

How very peaceful and comfortable it was to know that
people went into the ground like this to the accompani-
ment of singing and the sound of bells when they had
finished living.
Icelandic novelist **Halldór Laxness** *[1902–98], The Fish*
Can Sing, Chapter 12, 'A Good Funeral', 1957

Not all the preaching since Adam
Has made Death other than Death.
American poet **James Russell Lowell** *[1819–91],*
'After the Burial', in Under the Willows and Other Poems,
1868

Abide with me: fast falls the eventide;
The darkness deepens; Lord, with me abide;
When other helpers fail, and comforts flee,
Help of the helpless, O abide with me.

I fear no foe with thee at hand to bless;
Ills have no weight, and tears no bitterness.

Where is death's sting; where, grave, thy victory?
I triumph still, if thou abide with me . . .
Clergyman and hymnist **Henry Francis Lyte**
[1793–1847]

Everywhere she dies. Everywhere I go she dies.
No sunrise, no city square, no lurking beautiful mountain
but has her death in it.
The silence of her dying sounds through
the carousel of language, it's a web
on which laughter stitches itself. How can my hand
clasp another's when between them
is that thick death, that intolerable distance?
Scottish poet **Norman MacCaig** *[1910–96], 'Memorial',*
in The White Bird, 1973

God's heart was the first heart to break on that
Wednesday morning.
Scottish clergyman **Rev. Colin Mackintosh**, *minister of*
Dunblane Cathedral, in his sermon on 17 March 1996, on
the Dunblane Children's Massacre on 13 March 1996

There's nothing like a morning funeral for sharpening
the appetite for lunch.
Writer and entertainer **Arthur Marshall** *[1910–89],*
Life's Rich Pageant, 1984, it was quoted at his own pre-
lunch funeral

In my end is my beginning. – *En ma fin est mon commencement.*

   Mary, Queen of Scots *[1542–87]: motto embroidered by*
            her on her chair during her captivity in England

Dying is a very dull, dreary affair. And my advice to you is to have nothing whatever to do with it.

   Novelist and short-story writer **W Somerset Maugham**
   [1874–1965], to his nephew Robin Maugham, quoted in
                   Conversations with Willie, 1978

Down, down, down into the darkness of the grave
Gently they go, the beautiful, the tender, the kind;
Quietly they go, the intelligent, the witty, the brave.
I know. But I do not approve. And I am not resigned.
   American poet **Edna St Vincent Millay** *[1892–1950],*
         'Dirge without Music', in Buck in the Snow, 1928

One should always have one's boots on, and be ready to leave.
French essayist **Michel de Montaigne** *[1533–92], Essays,*
                                        1580

Like a prisoner awaiting his release, like a schoolboy when the end of term is near, like a migrant bird ready to fly south, like a patient in hospital anxiously scanning the doctor's face to see whether a discharge may be expected, I long to be gone. Extricating myself from the flesh I have too long inhabited, hearing the key turn in the lock of Time so that the great doors of Eternity swing open, disengaging my tired mind from its interminable conundrums and my tired ego from its wearisome insistencies. Such is the prospect of death.

Writer and broadcaster **Malcolm Muggeridge** *[1903–90]*

> Unfriendly friendly universe,
> I pack your stars into my purse,
> And bid you, bid you so farewell.

Orcadian poet **Edwin Muir** *[1887–1959], 'The Child Dying'*

> What passing-bells for these who die as cattle?
> Only the monstrous anger of the guns.
> Only the stuttering rifles' rapid rattle
> Can patter out their hasty orisons.

Poet **Wilfred Owen** *[1893–1918], 'Anthem for Doomed Youth', 1917*

This one's on me.

American writer and wit **Dorothy Parker** *[1893–1967]: suggested epitaph for her own tombstone, quoted in J Keats, You Might As Well Live, Part 1, Chapter 5*

Death is but crossing the World as Friends do the seas, they live in one another still.

Quaker and founder of Pennsylvania **William Penn** *[1644–1718]*

Dying
Is an art, like everything else.
I do it exceptionally well.

American poet **Sylvia Plath** *[1932–63], 'Lady Lazarus',*
1963

Death always comes too early or too late.

Proverb – *English*

Our last garment is made without pockets.

Proverb – *Italian*

O eloquent, just, and mighty Death! . . . thou hast drawn
together all the farstretched greatness, all the pride,
cruelty, and ambition of man, and covered it all over with
these two narrow words, *Hic jacet* (Here lies).

Mariner and courtier **Sir Walter Raleigh**
[c. 1552–1618], The History of the World, Preface,
1614

Remember me when I am gone away.
Gone far away into the silent land;
When you can no more hold me by the hand,
Nor I half turn to go yet turning stay.
Remember me when no more day by day
You tell me of our future that you planned:
Only remember me; you understand
It will be late to counsel then or pray.
Yet if you should forget me for a while
And afterwards remember, do not grieve:

For if the darkness and corruption leave
A vestige of the thoughts that once I had,
Better by far you should forget and smile
Than that you should remember and be sad.
Poet **Christina Rossetti** *[1830–94], 'Remember', 1862*

Waldo is one of those people who would be enormously
improved by death.
Scottish writer **Saki** *[H H Munro, 1870–1916],*
Beasts and Super-Beasts, 1914

There's rosemary, that's for remembrance; pray, love,
remember: and there is pansies, that's for thoughts.
Playwright **William Shakespeare** *[1564–1616], Hamlet,*
Act 4, Scene 5, Ophelia in grief, 'a document in madness'

Vex not his ghost: O! let him pass; he hates him
That would upon the rack of this tough world
Stretch him out longer.
Playwright **William Shakespeare** *[1564–1616], King Lear,*
Act 5, Scene 3, the Earl of Kent, about the dying King Lear

Nothing in his life
Became him like the leaving it: he died
As one that had been studied in his death
To throw away the dearest thing he ow'd
As 'twere a careless trifle.
Playwright **William Shakespeare** *[1564–1616],*
Macbeth, Act 1, Scene 4, Malcolm about the execution of
the thane of Cawdor

277

He hath awakened from the dream of life.
Poet **Percy Bysshe Shelley** *[1792–1822], Adonais, 1821,*
elegy on the death of John Keats

I cannot forgive my friends for dying; I do not find these
vanishing acts of theirs at all amusing.
American-born British writer **Logan Pearsall Smith**
[1865–1946], 'Age and Death', in Afterthoughts, 1931

Death must be distinguished from dying, with which it
is often confused.
Clergyman, writer and wit **Sydney Smith** *[1771–1845],*
quoted in Hesketh Pearson, The Smith of Smiths,
1934

Under the wide and starry sky
Dig the grave and let me lie.
Glad did I live and gladly die,
And I laid me down with a will.

This be the verse you grave for me:
'Here he lies where he longed to be;
Home is the sailor, home from sea
And the hunter home from the hill.'
Scottish writer **Robert Louis Stevenson** *[1850–94],*
'Requiem', in Underwoods, 1887; it is inscribed on his
gravestone on Mount Vaea, Samoa

The bitterest tears shed over graves are for words left unsaid and deeds left undone.

> *American writer and reformer* **Harriet Beecher Stowe**
> *[1811–96], Little Foxes, 1866*

If this is dying, then I don't think much of it.

> *Biographer and critic* **Lytton Strachey** *[1880–1932]*
> *on his deathbed; quoted in Michael Holroyd,*
> *Lytton Strachey, 1968*

God's finger touched him, and he slept.

> *Poet* **Alfred, Lord Tennyson** *[1809–92],*
> *In Memoriam A.H.H., 1850*

Though they go mad they shall be sane,
Though they sink through the sea they shall rise again;
Though lovers be lost, love shall not;
And death shall have no dominion.

> *Welsh poet and writer* **Dylan Thomas** *[1914–53],*
> *'And Death Shall Have No Dominion', 1936*

Some people are so afraid to die that they never begin to live.

> *American Presbyterian minister and writer*
> **Henry Van Dyke** *[1852–1933]*

Dear, beauteous death! the jewel of the just,
Shining nowhere but in the dark;
What mysteries do lie beyond thy dust,
Could man outlook that mark!
Poet **Henry Vaughan** *[1622–95], 'They are all gone',*
in Silex Scintillans, 1650–55

That was a good career move.
American novelist and critic **Gore Vidal** *[b. 1925]*
on hearing of the death of his friend and rival, Truman
Capote, in 1984

I know death hath ten thousand several doors
For men to take their exits.
Dramatist **John Webster** *[c. 1580–c. 1625], The Duchess*
of Malfi, Act 4, Scene 2, 1623